NHR/$13.50

THE SPRAY

THE SPRAY

Building and Sailing a Replica of Joshua Slocum's Famous Vessel

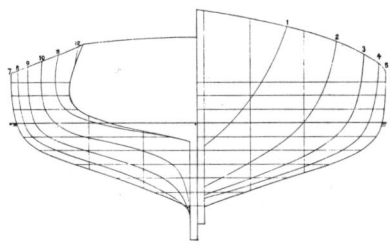

by R. D. Culler

*

International Marine
Publishing Company

Frontispiece—The Spray *after a day of sailing on Biscayne Bay, Florida, about 1940. (Photo by George Yater)*

Copyright © 1978
by International Marine Publishing Company
Library of Congress Catalog Card Number 78-55783
International Standard Book Number 0-87742-099-8

All rights reserved. Except for use in a review, no part of this book may be reproduced or utilized in any form or by any means, electronic or mechanical, including photocopying, recording, or by any information storage and retrieval system, without written permission from the publisher.

Typeset by A & B Typesetters, Inc., Concord, New Hampshire
Printed by Evans Printing Company, Concord, New Hampshire
Bound by New Hampshire Bindery, Concord, New Hampshire

Published by International Marine Publishing Company
21 Elm Street, Camden, Maine 04843

Contents

	Preface	vii
1	Introduction	1
2	Building the *Spray*	9
3	The *Spray*'s Performance	31
4	Above Decks	43
5	Below Decks	73
6	Upkeep	93
7	Living on Board	104
8	Some Conclusions	122
	Index	131

Preface

On first thought, it would seem of no value for me to write or you to read about my 23 years afloat as the builder and owner of a replica of Joshua Slocum's *Spray*, especially since the start of my life afloat was 48 years ago—50, if you consider the two years spent planning and dreaming. On second thought, it must be of interest, for I constantly get letters inquiring about the vessel. Most of these letter writers are apparently considering leading the life I once led, or something as close to it as changing times will allow—and times *have* changed since the times I describe.

There is no doubt that Slocum's voyage, writings, and vessel, the *Spray*, have been the cause of much argument, learned works, and some disparagement. In this book, I do not join in the arguing. Rather I describe what it was like to build and use my copy of Slocum's craft. The admirers of the *Spray* will look at her as they want to; the detractors the same. At this late date it is all water under the keel for me, and also for my wife, who became a part of my life afloat. What people think is no matter to us. All we can do is assure you that it was pretty good water while we were in it!

It seems there has always been a *Spray* replica being built somewhere in recent years—very recently there have been quite a few, of various materials and in various places. I often hear from the builders, the would-be builders, and those who are still just thinking about becoming builders. What I put down here is much of what I tell them. I hope it will be of interest and help to those about to build and sail a *Spray*, or more likely, those who will always just dream of doing it. I can assure those who are considering the task that it is work, and the road is long. But the undertaking is quite enjoyable if you are built for it, mentally more than physically.

There is no question that those building a *Spray* now, 48 years after I built mine, will have to do many things differently. Things were changing all the time I was at it—that's the way the world is. For all of this changing, I would still consider building my boat of wood, iron, and canvas, using the methods always used to build wooden boats. I am sure that part of my small success was that I had a sound craft—there was no experimentation with her construction. Properly handled, the vessel could not fail—her whole makeup has stood the test of time. It was up to those who manned her to make a go of it or not.

Looking back on our life with the *Spray*, we could have done better (and maybe not enjoyed it so much). All things considered, we did not do badly. The vessel herself? I think she was plain majestic.

R. D. Culler
Hyannis, Massachusetts

Publisher's Note

Pete Culler died not long before this book was published. We, his readers, are indeed fortunate that he took the time and trouble to sit down at the typewriter and share through the writing of three books and many articles his experience and wisdom relating to traditional vessels and small craft. His passing has made a void in the world of boats, but his writings make permanent at least the essence of his teachings on boatbuilding, sailing, and rowing. And surely people will have the good sense to build boats to his designs for a long time to come.

THE SPRAY

1 Introduction

Why did I build a replica of the *Spray* and determine to live my life afloat? I can't give a quick and easy answer to that anymore than can those of the present generation considering a life afloat. Yes, of course, romance was a factor. I think little really nice and interesting activity is accomplished without some romance. A few other considerations were no doubt independence, far horizons, trafficking with the sea, a simple life, depending upon one's own abilities, and many other small factors hard to define. Much of this could be found ashore, both in those days and now, for that matter. Some will now call it "a challenge," and some present thinking says we need such an ideal. In the times of my experience, this word was not used in the sense of today's meaning, at least not where I grew up.

I think I was mainly obeying the call of the sea, and man has been trying to explain this attraction since the beginning of seafaring—I can only add to past explana-

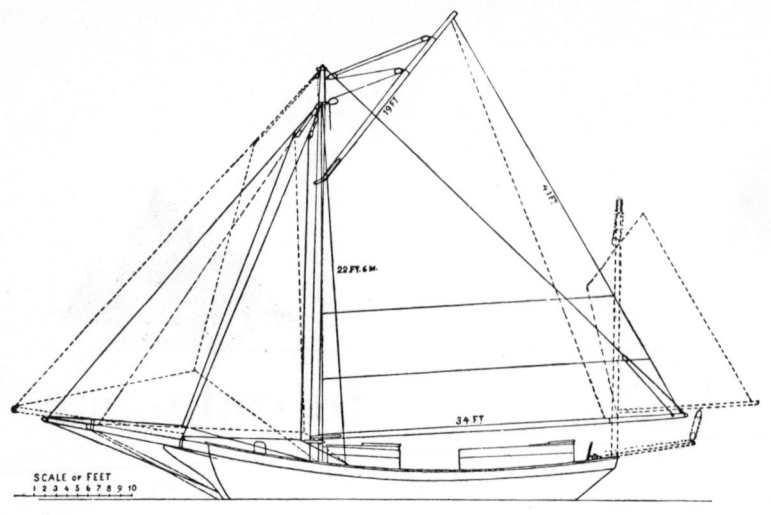

The Spray*'s sail plan, taken from Joshua Slocum's book,* Sailing Alone Around the World. *The solid lines show how she was rigged when she started the voyage, and the dotted lines show the modifications Slocum made during the cruise to make the rig easier to handle.*

tions by telling my story. If my readers find a little of the why in it, fine; if not, maybe I don't tell a good yarn.

I think a lot of my attraction to life afloat was caused by the vessel herself. Though I was very young when I started considering boat design, I was of the opinion that the *Spray* model was very well suited to the sea. This was caused by the brashness of youth, no doubt, but considerable use of the *Spray* and much subsequent experience in building and sailing other boats has not changed my opinion.

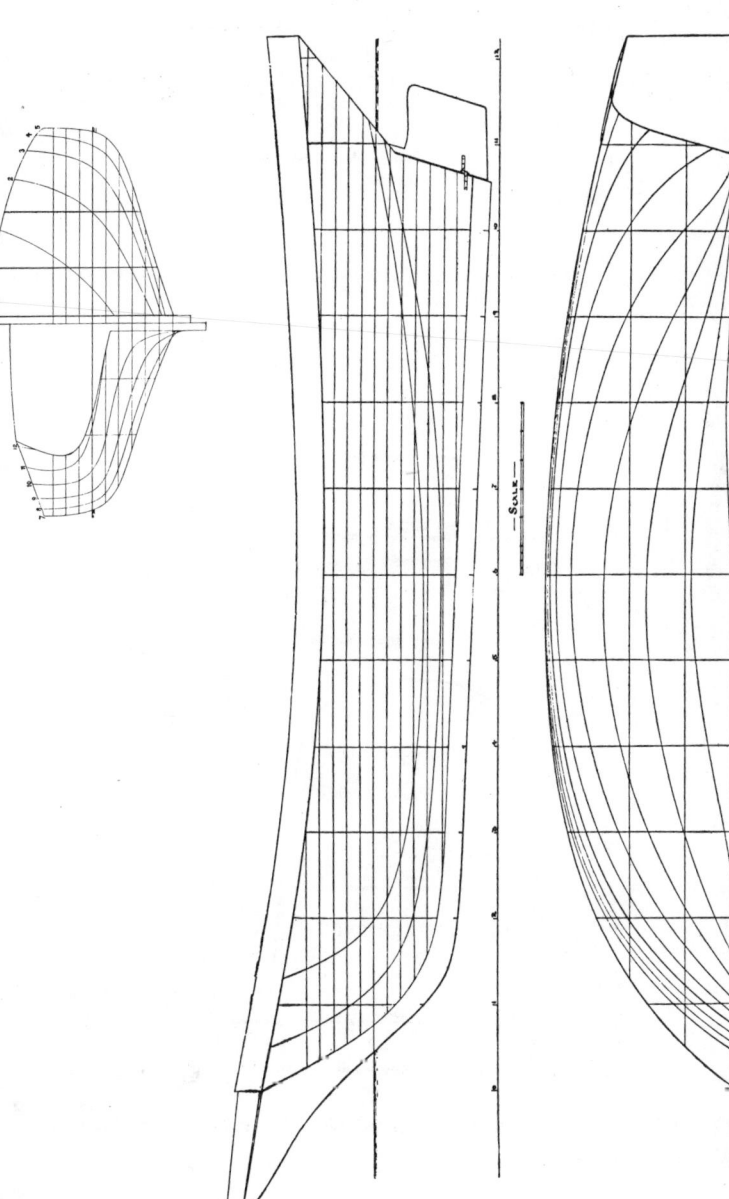

The Spray's lines as presented by Slocum in his book. They were drawn by Charles D. Mower from a model made by a Captain Robins from measurements he made from the Spray when she was hauled at his yard at Bridgeport, Connecticut, for the purpose.

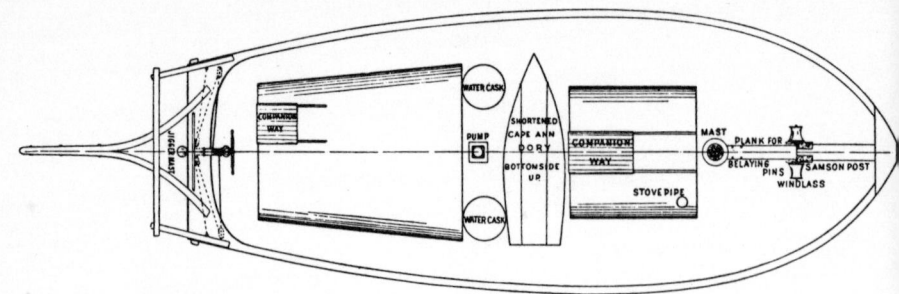

The Spray's *deck plan as shown in* Sailing Alone Around the World.

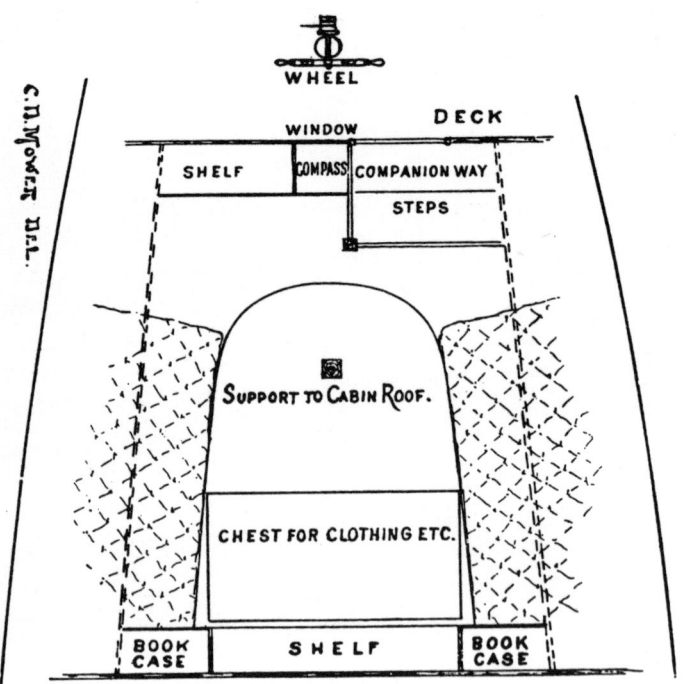

The plan of the Spray's *cabin shown in* Sailing Alone Around the World.

From an early age I was exposed to craft that would steer themselves, some better than others. *Spray*'s ability to do this was one of the factors that convinced me to build her. Even those who are most rabidly opposed to the *Spray*'s model must admit that for a boat to hold any course for long periods unattended is most useful. Among the usual run of craft, such a quality is quite rare. Now, it may be said that self-steering can be accomplished today on any boat by mechanical wind vanes and other new methods. This is possibly quite true most of the time, but the price is complexity. I believe that to be successful at sea we must keep things simple. My many reasons will be given as we go along, but I will give one reason right now—complexity means money, which was just as hard to come by in my day as it is now, maybe more so. Though banks lend people money to build boats now, such a practice was unheard of in my day. Boatbuilding and sailing were considered very high risk endeavors, and to my way of thinking, still are. You can lose all in a wink, insurance or no insurance.

But it was not self-steering alone that led me to the *Spray*. Another quality that attracted me was her good capacity. She would make a comfortable home in any climate, could carry plenty of stores and tools, and had room enough for other uses. I realized then as now that sailing is not totally cheap and free; a living must be made, and there are not many ways to make a living and sail, too.

One way to make a living is to work at a trade here and there. It has to be here and there, or you won't do any sailing. The shipwright's trade is a good one, as you need to know something of it anyway to acquire and maintain a vessel without having to rely on others more than you can afford.

At the time I began, chartering offered some chance to make money. Though to charter was not unusual, it was not at all organized in those days. As it turned out for me, the *Spray* was of a model that was quite suited to chartering in many ways. And there were other trades—it sometimes pays to learn more than one trade, at least learn them well enough so you can hold a job at them if you must. I've found that a man can nearly always find work anywhere if he's not too fussy.

My Dad always said that no matter what profession or other employment you might train for, always learn a trade, too—it might come in handy. I still think this is very good advice. I never lacked work when I needed it, even in the Great Depression, because I was willing, if not always knowing. One thing I did was dig blue clay at two bits an hour on "old drainer" tides to put a marine railway in, sometimes even at night—the tide is low in the dark, too. No overtime, no fringe benefits—here's a shovel, work if you want it, pay in cash, no taxes. Terrible? Second-class citizen? Maybe. Wages were low, but a haircut was two bits, there were three grades of coffee in the store at 15, 19, and 21 cents a pound, and, once in a while when a tough job was pulled off very well, we were treated to a slug of the local 'shine.

Sometimes things were grim, and I would wonder if there would be much sailing ahead in the future. But the vessel was always kept up, and was even in the winter at the near-ready. Early chartering was extremely slow, on account of the times and my lack of knowledge of how to go about things. The thing was that I stuck to it— possibly because I did not have sense enough to do otherwise. I long ago found that if you have something to offer, even though it is not very much, just as long as it's sound, and if you hang with it long enough, people will finally begin to notice. You will be on your way.

The *Spray*, and what I had done with her, had something, and it was eventually noticed and used. I later had the satisfaction of seeing what had been ridicule in some quarters turn to envy. We even got so successful (in a very small way) that we were blackballed a couple of times, of which more later.

I can't say that I took to the sea as a form of escape; I had nothing to escape from. You hear of various people "escaping from it all" by going to sea, heading for the woods, or taking some other avenue to get away from the rat race, etc. I never felt that way, being of the type who even now is satisfied with his lot. Once I was well established, I met many who thought it was a fine means of escape—from something, I'm not sure what. It has been my experience that if you "escape" from one thing you become entrapped by another. As I think back, the only time I was unhappy about things for long periods was during the war years, and millions of others were, too. Yet even those times had some good points, if you can call anything about wartime good.

Yes, I think it was just the sea calling, and there is no better time to heed its call than when you are young. Just how you do it will be very much based on the times you find yourself in. Looking back on it, trying to get a start in the famous Depression was not easy, though it did not seem hard at the time. Maybe it was the best time—there was nowhere else to go but up. Yes, do it young, while you have plenty of fire and strength; you get it hot off the stove and are quite able to cope with difficulty. What does it matter, for instance, if you have a 30-hour stint, more or less on duty the whole time? You can take it.

I think there is nothing sadder and more frustrating to a builder and designer than to create a nice craft for someone in his sixties, who has made his pile and can now afford the best, and who is full of the ailments of age. The craft of his dreams is complicated and must have a hired skipper, and the owner never really gets to know her or gain real enjoyment from what he's quite able to afford. Maybe his "position in life" and how he hopes he looks in the eyes of his peers is worth it, but, at the risk of a bad pun, I say he missed the boat!

On the other hand, one who starts young and follows boats as a way of life always seems quite happy in his dotage. When such a person feels the weight of time, he knows full well he can't go aloft or tussle with a big mainsail or engage in all the other exciting things of his youth. He can do as I do—fool around the shore in some little boat. He will have wonderful memories to go with her.

Why did I build a replica of the *Spray* and determine to live my life afloat? I'll let you draw your own conclusions.

2 Building the Spray*

After I decided to build the *Spray*, some study was given to locations for building, timber, and men skilled in constructing such a craft and in shipbuilding in general. Around 1929, there were many yards with skilled men on the East Coast; however, a part of the country where the economics were suited to the type of craft was very important. The model was not a type suited to or needing the skills of such as Lawley or Nevins.

The Eastern Shore of Chesapeake Bay was chosen, and Oxford, Maryland, a very small village devoted to the oyster trade, was picked. After all, the old *Spray*

---

*This chapter, in a slightly different form, was originally published in the author's book *Skiffs and Schooners* (International Marine Publishing Company, Camden, Maine, 1974).

Above: *Alonzo R. Conley, the master builder at the yard at Oxford, Maryland, where the replica of the* Spray *was built. (Courtesy Mrs. James Conley and the Mariner's Museum, Newport News, Virginia.)* Below: *The shipyard in Oxford, Maryland, where the* Spray *was built. The oyster trade, evidenced by the oyster dredgers in the background, was the mainstay of this small, Eastern Shore community.*

was considered by some folks to be "only an old oyster boat," so what better set-up? The community at the time was said, by those who knew, to be very much like small New England coastal villages in about 1870. There were great changes just around the corner, however, and in a very few short years all was different. Progress caught up, and, to my way of thinking, the place was spoiled forever.

The master builder, Alonzo R. Conley, was a man of much skill and long experience. He had several large vessels to his credit, both in design and building. He was willing to take me on as a learning apprentice; what I produced I saved on the vessel. Let it be said he was a fine teacher. Though of small formal education, this man had a vast working knowledge of his trade and was quite familiar with many of the older written works on the subject; he promptly lent me some classic books on shipbuilding.

The business arrangement was simple, and one that I still find good for a builder who really knows his stuff and a client who is honest about his own finances. The arrangement was this: The builder thought the vessel "would not cost over so much." He was right; she was a little less. The work on her was not to interfere with the seasonal work required on the oyster fleet and freighters, most of these still being sailing vessels, though some were cargo power craft. There would be slack periods on my vessel on this account, when I would go it alone when and where I was able. Payment was to be so much a month; sometimes I was ahead, sometimes behind, but for the most part it ran pretty even, and no one was hurt.

There was plenty of good timber. This was white oak country, and hard pine was available in balks from "the city." White cedar came in by boat, and in those days yards stocked ahead. Hardware was no problem, or sails either, as there were both shipsmith and sailmaker right next door.

The yard layout was about what was customary then. There was sloping land to a creek and anchorage, with several big shade trees and plenty of room, two railways, and space to set up three or more new vessels. The main building was a stark old post-and-rail affair, framed with local gum wood so hard with age it would refuse a nail, sheathed with vertical boards, battened, and covered with a ternplate roof. The building was the traditional ochre color. One small corner was the office and store room and had wonderful smells. The other end was the mill, which had a shipsaw and planer only, these being the total machinery and both very old. The rest of the lower floor was devoted to work benches, tool boxes, and space to work timber or build a motor yawlboat. Large sliding doors were in many places in the building, so there was always a clear shot for getting big timber to the machines.

There was a loft upstairs for laying down and a small room off it for oakum and for storing the large jeer blocks (each filling a wheelbarrow) and fall used to rig the big sheer legs on the end of the dock. (A wooden, walk-around capstan was near the sheers.) At the other end of the loft was a home-built wood lathe of large capacity, driven by a tiny hopper engine that was quite short-tempered on a cold morning.

Outside, the yard had a cluttered and messy look by some standards, for there was much work going on. There would be time enough to clean up when things were slack. Winters were cold, and there was much need of firewood. Much good ship timber was about, piled everywhere, and carefully "stuck." There were timber wheels, peaveys, many clamps, some of them huge, and, of course, "planking jacks." The railways were driven by locally made, single-cylinder hit-and-miss, gas engines, cooled by toted creek water kept in pickle barrels. These engines were rated at 5 h.p. each. There was the outhouse, which hung over the end of a bulkhead at a rakish angle. It was fearsomely cold or hot inside it, depending on the season, but it never needed maintenance. There was no electricity at all in the yard, though the owner's house next door and most of the village had it, made locally, as was the custom then. Hand-held power tools were unknown. Water for drinking came from the ice house next door, where it ran in a fine cool stream. Each workman went for his own water with a "can," which was really a half-gallon mason jar of the bootleg era.

How, many folks ask now, can you build a vessel with such a crude setup? You can, and they did, and, sad to say, the man-hours per ton of vessel then were less, sometimes very much less, than they are now. Lest you might think the work was crude, let me say it was just the opposite. The yard was known for the fair hulls, fine planking, and excellence of fastening on the craft it turned out. There seemed to be no great effort to accomplish this; all hands just knew how.

Everyone walked to work, for the village was small, few people owned autos, and all was geared to the yards and oyster trade. You worked at what the place offered, or left for greener fields. Few left. There were few amusements; we didn't need any, for the country store was the men's social place. For yarns of hard sailings, great feats of hunting, gossip, lies, and all sorts of exciting things, you went to the store evenings. The layout was just like the pictures of a real country store. The smoke got pretty thick (many of the men smoked black Five Brothers) and things got pretty deep, but we all wore boots!

Looking back on it, knowing there were what would now be considered great discomforts, it was still a good way to live, maybe because we did not know any better. To hear "Captain Harry" get going and take the floor for a full evening (being baited now and then to keep it hot) was a far better show than any purveyors of the boob tube can put on now!

Grub was hearty; oysters in many forms were commonplace at the table, cooked by experts. Nowadays, oysters cost a fortune, and the cooks louse 'em up. A breakfast of biscuits, or "corn cake and aigs" with fried fatback was fit to do hard work on. The dinner bucket carried solid food, too. There were no thermos bottles; coffee was brought in an ordinary bottle and cuddled close to the office stove in winter so it was just right at noon. Sometimes it almost froze on the way to work. In summer, and it can be frightfully hot on the Bay, the kindly engineer in charge of the nearby ice house made ice tea or coffee commonplace. You could even have it frozen if you wanted. Working hours were longer than they are now, based on available daylight. There were no rules for workmen, no regulations, except what the Master made. This was the pre-Roosevelt era, and the yard was fairly isolated from city ways. There was no insurance of any kind, no guards on the belts, no fire equipment. It was probably not much different from, say, a farm a hundred years ago. Everyone knew his work, and accidents or mishaps of any kind were most rare.

A yard must have a crew of workmen; this crew was small and was supplemented at times of much work by some old timers from what had once been a very active shipbuilding area farther down the Bay. These fellows came for a specific job, saw it through, and departed to return later on for some other project. They were highly skilled, experienced in large work, and could pretty much run any job without supervision. The boss of this little yard was shown considerable deference by these seasoned old timers, though he was younger than they, for he had once been a designer and builder in the Big Time, and these men had been under him. He had something they lacked.

The regular crew were, as they always are, varied in looks, build, and personality. The common trait was that they knew their work and very much knew that the Master Shipwright knew his. There was Hamilton, a leathery, sparse man of excellent ability in all phases of his trade, besides being an accomplished rigger. Edward, who was black, though his head was quite white, was no doubt much older than he looked. Caulker and fastener extraordinary, he lent magic to a pin maul with his hands. Isaac, short, round, and strong, though his legs were giving out, had a Santa Claus face without the whiskers. He could dub and hew accurately with the dispatch of a machine, and from the most impossible positions. In his retirement years, he kindly sold me one of his fine adzes for one dollar. I've used it for years, and still do occasionally. The bell-like ring that is its trademark is still with it!

Tom was addicted to bad whiskey; it was an unwritten rule that he was not to show up when in bad shape. To make up for his tardiness, he would turn out at one o'clock in the morning, if necessary, to man the railway to haul some leaking craft that was about to go down. Going overboard in the total darkness of a winter night to find out what was ailing a sticking poppet bothered him not at all. Wedges, clamps, jacks, and all sorts of heavy work was his specialty. Tom was not very robust looking, probably couldn't see out of one eye, and was racked by demon rum, but none of these ailments seemed to cramp his style any.

Edgar, somewhat younger than the others, was the foreman. He kept time for all and rang the old, dismal, cracked bell for starting work and knocking off. He generally kept the run of the others' work and did most of the spiling and laying off, once a job was started. Edgar maintained the mill and engines, for which he had a great knack. He set and filed the miles of bandsaw blades. He did most of the interior joinerwork, including fine, paneled doors. There was no small machinery for joinerwork; it was all done by hand, rapidly, and in good style. Edgar owned a Stanley 55 plane, "a joiner shop in itself," if you get behind it and push! Besides all this, he was a sawyer, and a wizard at it.

So money was passed, and I was put to work in the loft with a broom. Then I was introduced to the fine points of lofting, many of which seem not to be found in books. I flattened the points of hundreds of thin wire nails. Though the floor was old and dark, it was treated with respect. The flattened points left little or no holes and had other advantages. Much work was done with chalk, and I learned you can work quite accurately to chalk lines, once shown how. I also learned what "fair" is, a thing many of the highly skilled can still argue about. A master can show you just what a very slight adjustment can do for a line that seems good already. I learned about lifting the bevels, for my vessel was to be a sawn-frame craft. I had never seen a bevel-lifting instrument; no shipbuilding books I've seen show such a thing. The Master had built it. I've since built one and have had it for a good many years. I learned mould making; the whole backbone and all the frames had moulds, for this was all gone about as if she were a big four-master. This is, in the end, the fastest, most accurate way to build a sawn-frame vessel.

Nailed on one wall, looking down on all this, was the profile and sail plan of a fine four-masted schooner, the past work of my designer-builder-teacher. She had made some maritime history as "The Ship The Sea Couldn't Kill." Her sails and all spars and rigging were made from this plan; it was drawn in pencil on common matchboarding. Men of these skills got right at the heart of the matter without the frills of offices, tidy draftsmen, and much paperwork, and they never failed to be artistic in their work.

There was plenty of stock on hand for framing. During the lofting, a most battered truck came with the keel, stem, and deadwood stock from a backwoods mill by some swamp. All mill trucks were battered, but this one was special. The mill owner unfolds from the cab, an elderly Mennonite in the garb of his sect. Immediate haggling follows between shipwright and mill owner, as, though both are good churchmen, neither trusts the other's lumber tally. Some Eastern Sho' white oak won't float when green, and, while the haggle proceeds, a huge giant, unshorn since birth, unloads this great pile in short order, singlehanded, with a peavey and a simple (so it seems) twist of the wrist. He's an astonishing fellow. He thinks maybe he's thirty-six years old. His boss says he has eighteen children. It's rumored that he lives in a true serfdom under this small lumber baron.

This timber is soon converted. There is much screeching from the ancient bandsaw and bellowing from the engine. Both are quite up to it and labor not at all. There is considerable adz work, rabbet cutting, drifting, and then setting up. The mysteries of setting to drag and plumbing up were fully explained, doing it in a wind, too! The ground where the backbone was set up was traditional to these yards, a hardpacked, unknown depth of adz and axe chips from 125 years of building by various men on the same site. The old railways had seen all kinds of power. First a horse walk-around, then steam, now gasoline engines.

It was soon time to frame up, and getting cold. The oyster season was well started and all the craft were on the beds. Framing is an all-hands job. The Master

Above: *The white oak keel and shoe are the first timbers to be laid down.* Below: *Alonzo Conley, the master builder, moulding the frame. Patterns taken from the lofting are laid down on the white oak flitches, and the proper shapes are marked off.*

The white oak backbone set up. Those are sawn frames in the foreground.

moulded. Much flitch was spread around for his easy access. The timber wheels were much in use. As he moulded, the work was taken to the saw. Four-inch white oak flitch is heavy.

To this day I very much enjoy the sawing of frame for a vessel. Usually there is a cold wind sweeping across the huge saw table. There is the heady smell of new-sawn oak, the rumble of rollers as the flitch is jockeyed into position to start the cut. There is the idling saw, veteran of a billion cuts, and the loafing engine, sounding sort of slack in the rod. The saw is rolled down to the proper starting bevel, the motions from the sawyer's hand guiding the crew in lining her up, and the roller crank is then rigged. And the cut starts, hesitantly at first, then, as she's lined up, the big saw cuts in earnest, and the machinery and crew settle into stride. With gentle motions occasionally from the sawyer's hand, the saw gradually lays back more and more as the bevel increases. There is much sawdust in the eyes, as it's windy, and an occasional spark from the saw guides. It's through, the tempo of the machine slacks off again, the bevel man stands her up and she rumbles back to get the other side.

If it's a cant frame with rapidly changing shape and bevel, things can become quite tense. The bevel man can only just keep up with the changes and cranks the wheel for all he's worth. Usually the sharpest curve is at one end, when the crew is carrying most of the weight of the timber. The sawyer's signals become somewhat rapid, the old saw is almost lying on its back, a stream of sparks strikes from the blade, she whines and yammers, there is a hysterical shriek from the drive belt with much slapping, and the old engine thumps manfully. Then she's through, right on the line. There's little dubbing to do with this kind of work.

Yes, it gets in the blood, and though modern ship saws have improved slightly, with their heavy, solid lower wheels to act as a flywheel and their swage-tooth blades, driven by five vee belts connected to quiet electric motors that need no water or gas toted by hand for them, there is little other change. New-sawn oak smells the same, and the saw blade has the same screech. I am glad to have heard the fine slap of the big, totally exposed, flat belts and the bark of a steam mill exhaust when the engine's governor said "go to work," and to have seen the drunken rocking of the big upright gas engines when they were Laying Into It. Wooden shipbuilding sounds and smells good!

Framing up took just a week; this sounds fantastic to many folks who have not experienced such things. Men who knew their trade, rugged though very simple equipment just suited to such work, and a vessel of only 15 tons made this possible. The fact that she was framed much heavier than usual for a craft of her length made no difference; the same motions had to be gone through. The main reason for the heavy framing was that the vessel is of a naturally weak shape and maybe overly stiff, so it seemed well to build some of the ballast into her. Much subsequent use proved this approach.

There was a coaster waiting her fate anchored off the yard. Old and worn with work, she was a sad sight, with drooping stern and other signs of a hard life. It was suddenly decided to rebuild her, as at this time there was a local economic reason to rebuild old vessels, some being converted to power. It later turned out that this was the last big effort at this sort of thing on the Bay.

As the schooner job was urgent, it was decided to let the *Spray* frame set for the winter, and "find and set" itself, to be horned and trued again when work started on her later. I still think this is a good practice; it was once common in first-class housebuilding, too. "Lets the snow work the sap out."

I was put to work on deck beams, beams for the cabin trunk, parts for hatches, and spars, all under the Master's direction. Prefab was well understood here. I went alone, mostly in the old drafty loft, the ternplate roof rattling dismally to winter Nor'westers that turned the river "feather white."

Meanwhile, the schooner was hauled on the big railway and prepared for her major operation. This in itself was quite a project, salted with much know-how. Her ends were knocked out, and most of her topwork taken off to the waterline. Old bottoms usually are in good shape, except for the ends. Her deck was cut loose from her sides with her masts still in her. She was all jacked, shored, and stayed to deadmen buried in the yard, of which there were many, some dating back to the beginning. I had an excellent view of all of this from the loft, for the vessel was right below me, with her headstays secured to the head of the railway. I began to realize I was witnessing The Big Time, a master shipwright at his best. The battered mill truck and the giant were frequent visitors with huge piles of oak. The stem liner, otherwise known as an apron piece, arrived. It was a noble chunk, 18 inches x 24 inches x 20 feet. Isaac, the axe wizard, was put on it, and some of the days were so cold it's a wonder his axe stood it.

The old timers from Down the Bay showed up, all of 'em, and boarded locally in the village during the working week. Captain Bill, framer-planker-ceiler extraordinary, was sort of chief, under the Master. His hands were so big that cotton work gloves covered only a little more than half of them. John, aged 74, who "could lay off work for 25 head of men and do a full day's work besides," could and did! His brother, 72 and hunchbacked, had a 42-inch handle in his maul and could do anything with it. No one else could do a thing with the tool. It was just too long. Pap, who was supposed to be 84, was so shrunken and withered it was said he had a brick in each pocket to keep from blowing away, yet he was right in it with the rest. There were a couple of younger men making up, with the yard steadies, quite a crew.

The mill roared, and the old building creaked with its efforts, as all the strain was transmitted to the frame through the big overhead line shaft. I heard the ring of pin mauls, the chunking of adz and axe, and the constant rumble of rollers moving heavy stuff. Then a sick cruiser showed up, and this job was taken on. One of the younger men from Down the Bay was put to "opening her up." The Master stopped by daily to check my lone progress, and he seemed satisfied. One day he said, "Harly needs help on the cruiser." Would I give him a hand? I was part of the crew the rest of the winter, and the cruiser turned out well after we gave her a new stem and replanked her topwork. Harly knew considerable about yacht planking.

By early spring the schooner was about finished. Soon she was launched. She had the yard's handsome, springy sheer and was every inch a smart coaster. Her new master had been by her all winter. A thorough seaman and somewhat of a dude (always wore a store suit), he was a stickler for doing it right, and she was properly rigged and fitted out in record time. One day she sailed, in half a gale. She made a short board across the creek, went about with much volleying from the new canvas, and then she was standing down river, leaving "a wake as wide as the State Road."

The *Spray*'s hull in frame was worked on as the oyster fleet's spring repairs allowed, and, as it got warm, planking and ceiling started in earnest. A steam box was, of course, used, as hard pine is stiff, and the curves were full. Right here I learned about ceiling run and planking run, too, things which seem to be overlooked in books and seem to have been forgotten. Later on, in the World War II years, this fact began immediately to show up. In that era, I suddenly found myself as Boss Planker "with twenty-nine head of men under me," a most successful one, they said, and I lay it all to the teaching of those who really knew.

Soon beams were going into the *Spray*, and waterways, decks, and the trunk were started. When she was about together on top, it was time to think of getting her tight so work could go on below in bad weather, for fall storms were not far away. It was time to caulk her hull, too. Edward, the caulker, got a couple of his crew from the old days from Down the Bay, and they went at it. This was quite a show in itself. Caulking was a trade of its own and took much learning. Morning starts were slow and hesitant, especially if it was a bit chilly. Then

Planking with hard pine is underway.

The hard pine ceiling going in. The vertical member back aft is the rudder casing. The transom is white oak.

The white oak deck framing in place. Note the knightheads up forward.

the tempo would increase slightly, the magic black hands feeding the cotton and oakum like machines. There would come a moan from somewhere under her, an answering hum, and shortly a hymn would start, lightly at first, in time with the mallets. Each mallet had a voice of its own. The tempo would increase, with much punctuation from the mallets. The crab pickers next door would pick up the hymn, and soon there would be a real old rouser going. At some mystic signal from the boss mallet, all would stop; at a cry from it another would start, a real old foot-stomper this time! By then, the sun would be beating down, happy looks were on the shiny black faces, and the real fun would start. Suddenly all mallets would stop but one, he would solo with much art and many flourishes, and then the chorus would come in again, until some other would do his solo. This went on all day until she was caulked; no wonder it did not take long.

I asked Edward how it was in the days of the big vessels. His face lighted up. "When 'e done the *White*, had a thick oak bottom, first-class seams, and twenty head of men under her. Man, that were Music!" He was referring to the four-master, the *Purnell T. White*. My vessel was, of course, tight, and stayed so. Fifteen years later she was "set back" for the first time. Ancient Ed was still around, though others did the job. I had consulted him about it, and he thought "it was about time."

Deck details were worked on as the weather allowed, and, as it was getting cool, the stove was set up below. On bad days, we built the cabin around it. Simple though attractive, it was a vessel's cabin. Then there was much bunging and painting outside, with much effort on the seams, which were all rodded back. She sat at the edge of a bulkhead near the sheers. A big November tide was needed, as otherwise there was quite a drop and not much water ordinarily.

The line of the launching just cleared the old backhouse. It was a true shipways launching, on grease, as that was the custom, even for very small vessels. Ways were built, and she had the customary trial packing. Then, as the day approached, tallow was heated, the ways greased, stops rigged, and the whole thing repacked. Launching day was cold and raw with little wind. The tide came well, as there was a gale in the offing. The bulkhead was cut down in way of the keel passage in case the ways settled; no one wanted any toe-stubbing. There was no check line, as the creek was wide, the vessel small, and what wind there was would drift her back to the dock.

This was an honest saw-off launching. The wedges were driven to raise her, the keel blocks were knocked

The hull is closed in. The decks are hard pine; the house top is cedar.

The seams are caulked and payed. Launching time is near.

The ways are rigged for launching.

out, and she bore on the sliding ways. The dogs were tripped, the tide lapped the bulkhead, and the order was given to start the big crosscuts, just sharpened for this occasion. Halfway through came an order to stop; the Master measured each side. Then he said, "Cut her off," and they did. She sat. Edward dropped his end of the saw, faced the vessel, and salaamed mightily, speaking in some strange lingo. A rumble went through the whole structure and she started, slowly at first, then with a rapid increase, a Splash, and much popping up of spewed blocks. A blue cloud appeared at the end of the ways; the tallow had smoked, so it was a proper launching. She was warped in to the dock, the pump was tried, and she was well made fast, for there was wind coming.

The Spray *slides down the ways and is afloat.*

The Spray *undergoing her first fitout.*

The cabin stove felt fine, for we had been "keeping fire" now for several days. Tomorrow was Thanksgiving, and to hell with the mess of battered ways for this week. Those that used it had something to take home and warm up with, for all hands were chilled through. Even a small launching can be an exhausting business. The vessel was checked as to water late that night, and the next morning the pump was frozen. What matter? She did not need it.

The rest was routine: masting, rigging, trials, and many years of sailing in good weather and bad, many ups and downs. More of this later. Her construction never let her down. I had her a long time, and she has not had very many owners since. Rumor a short while ago had it she's still afloat and is for sale at many, many times her first cost. At 23, when I parted with her, she was quite sound. Now, I don't know. Like many of us getting along, she might well "have considerable dote."

3 The Spray's Performance

Once the *Spray* was built and sailing, I was constantly asked, "How does she sail?" and before I could answer that, "How does she go to windward?" This last question always seemed to be of the utmost importance, even to those who did most of their sailing in books. My usual answer was, "About like any coaster." This was always most unsatisfactory to my questioners, because none of these people knew how a coaster sailed. So it all had to be explained in detail, which again was not satisfactory, as those asking could not imagine that great windward ability was of small matter to me. After all, windward ability is only one of many things that make up a useful vessel.

No vessel based on the design of a working craft will sail by the wind like some craft designed totally for closed-course racing. There is no need of it. This last is not hard to understand when you consider crew fatigue. Both working craft and cruising craft based on working

A fine day for sailing. Note the absence of a cockpit.

craft models do not make long treks to windward simply because it is not worth it—the crew gets all tired out. The Lord gave us wits to learn how to work the wind systems, and you do this even when coasting—you wait a "chance along," a term that the old coasters well understand. It means a favorable wind, something worth waiting for.

On the other hand, my *Spray* was in some ways very good to windward, as she could slug. She did not point close, or foot fast, but my, how she could stick to it when the chips were down. When things got really hairy, she could out-carry any yacht type she met. She often gave the impression of outpointing them, when in fact they were heeled so much that their leeway was very great; with this much wind she did foot quite fast.

She could put up one hell of a battle on a lee shore, and, up to now, has always won. A vessel with this ability will not tolerate weak gear; she can punish it if you call on all she has in her. This applies to the hull construction, too—a vessel of great power requires construction to go with it. Those who have not sailed such craft have no conception of their power to carry sail. That power must be understood and handled correctly—it can get out of hand with mismanagement.

This brings up another question, related to sail-carrying ability: "Will she capsize?" I don't know. All I can say is that she never did, and she never even slightly indicated she could be inclined that way. This often led to yet another question: "Does she have outside ballast?" The answer is no, which often ended the discussion. If the discussion went further, it was, and still is, hard to get across that the model is totally unsuited to outside ballast, and such ballast would be harmful to her motion.

The real meat of my *Spray*'s sailing ability, passage-making, was little understood, too. That she was an excellent passagemaker, as was Slocum's original, is often beside the point to many in these discussions. I consider the model fast in passagemaking, and here is why: She ran a very true course, could be pushed hard—yet would be under excellent control—and had no tendency to cause a following sea to break. She left a very flat wake with no quarter wave. Having an easy motion seemed to help; a rough sea did not slow her down.

If one has sense enough to use the wind systems to the fullest, and has a vessel able to take what they dish out, fast passages will be standard, with any luck at all. In fact, in the years when she was well known on the coast, many said she seemed always to be driving along under a press of sail in a strong, fair wind, which, in a way, was so; we simply took advantage of a good slant. The *Spray* made many passages in a day or two or three. The same passages took other vessels weeks, because they started at the wrong end of a wind system. With

The key to the Spray's sailing ability was to take advantage of a good slant. This photograph gives a view of the robustness of her rig.

the *Spray*'s ability to go in most anything, as long as it was fair, she seemed to others to be very fast at times. To cap it all, she did her driving in a way that allowed reasonable comfort with regular meals—this, in itself, is something many craft just can't do.

The kind of sailing we did was almost always with a small crew, and, sometimes, from necessity, singlehanded. I have sailed singlehanded considerably and don't really recommend it. Avoid it if you can. But if you must go alone, an easy handling and docile vessel is needed, or you will wear out quickly. Look for a craft with an easy motion and get food and rest regularly; all of this is more nearly possible in a boat such as the *Spray* than in the usual run of cruising craft. In fact, I look on what some now consider to be good cruising boats as totally unfit for the life we led in the past. To arrive at this conclusion, I have considered handling, motion, storage, upkeep, and a host of other characteristics.

The way of life I speak about has not changed any once you are clear of the land; on the other hand, once you get a line ashore, or even drop an anchor in some cases, things are different from what they were forty some years ago. These shoreside differences, not offshore considerations, have caused changes in cruising boats. Whether this is really good or not, I don't know. I do know that I don't like most of it, for it tends to get you away from simplicity. Simple things are usually cheaper and are more easily kept in repair.

I think a great part of a vessel's sailing ability is more than just being able to go through the water fast; she should do it easily, with modest strain on the gear and crew, at least in average weather. Even the ease of sail handling is very much dependent on a craft that sails well. And what is important is not so much the size of the gear, but how well designed it is for the purpose.

Above: *Sailing full and by off Fort Lauderdale, Florida.* Opposite, top: *A bone in her teeth.* Opposite, bottom: *Lifting to it. (Photos by George Yater)*

The Spray *was a comfortable boat to sail. Note the water cask up forward against the rail.*

    I have sailed many different boats, some fast by yachting standards, and have designed a number, but I still think that, for an all-around cruising craft, the *Spray* model is a good sailer, exceptional in some ways. You do have to learn how to give her the breaks to set her free, and when you do, she knows what to do. I must emphasize, however, that as a week-ender, with the usual two-week vacation cruise so many people have to be satisfied with, I say no, the *Spray* is quite unfit.

    It will be noticed by those who have followed my design work that little, if any, of my work has been influenced by the *Spray* model. This is simply because I prefer to design for a certain use and waters as much as possible. The design requirements suited to the *Spray* seldom come up, and if they do, I simply say, use her model—why make another, when I don't know how to improve on it?

Another common question I heard about the *Spray* concerned her sea-keeping ability. Just why this would be questioned at all, in the light of Slocum's record in the boat, I don't know. But people always asked, and I always answered. I'll tell you about the *Spray*'s sea-keeping ability simply as I found it.

To begin with, the vessel had a very easy motion, as mentioned before. This easy motion, in itself, usually indicates a rather good seaboat. I've studied the centers of oscillation of many craft underway, simply for my own interest. My craft's point was slightly above the cabin table and very near the mid frame, and it seemed to shift little or none in all conditions of sea and sailing. Or to put it simply, she was somewhat famous for not throwing things and people about in a seaway. This cannot be said of many craft. Sailing with a big sea abeam, she seemed easier than any other craft I've been in. She slid to leeward just enough and came back with no whip, and for all the dogma of full bows making a boat gripe, the *Spray* did not do so. Why this is so, I'm not sure. Her lines have been put to all sorts of study, yet the answers still don't seem clear. The experts talk of "perfect balance," yet I don't think she had perfect balance by modern design standards. By her own design standards, she has us all mystified. None of it makes much sense if we go by The Book, as preached now.

You just don't suppose The Book could be in error in some ways?

The *Spray* was quite a dry boat; solid water aboard was most rare. When forced hard by the wind, she could live up to her name almost any craft will throw spray if pushed hard. Actually my boat threw very little, and

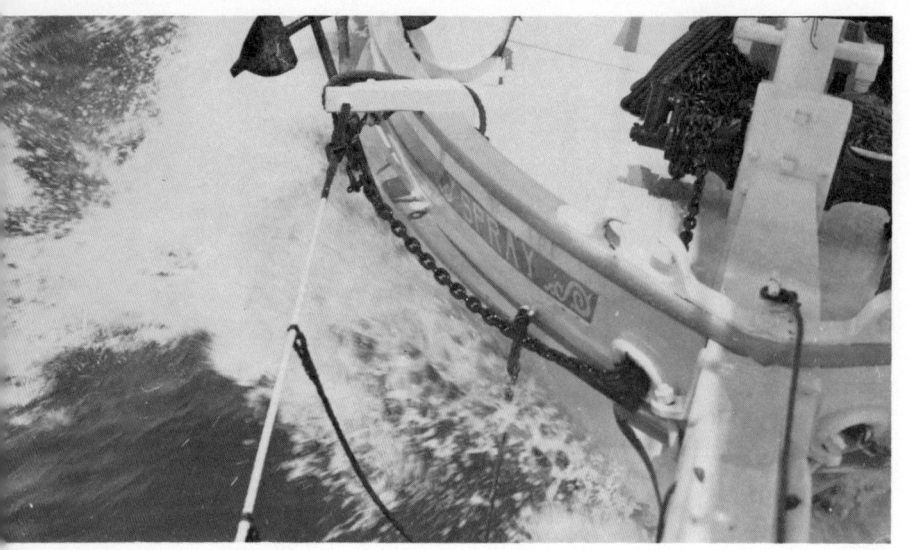

The Spray *threw some of what she was named for, but little came aboard because of her high bulwarks. We almost never took solid water on deck.*

what she did throw was more a fine mist than anything else. What little water came aboard quickly left, as the shape of the craft tended not to hold it.

Some say deep bulwarks on a vessel are unsafe, as they hold a lot of water. This is perhaps true in some very big craft, under certain conditions, such as when they are loaded with cargo. Small vessels simply roll the water off. *Spray* might have had bulwarks, but she had no cockpit, none being needed in such a craft. This alone is a great advantage. There are good cockpits, but many more bad ones. If you don't need one, don't have it; you will avoid many headaches. Many now just can't imagine any boat without a cockpit. Until you have experienced being without—of course in a craft that does not need one—you cannot possibly know the joys of a cockpit-less boat.

Underway, displaying her most endearing quality—self-steering.

I know that few will agree with me here, as most believe that boat and cockpit mean almost the same thing. My long-held opinion on cockpits is that they are a necessary abomination on most smaller craft, a pain to the designer, more of a pain to the builder, a harbor for rot and dirt, and a possible leg breaker. All this adds up to expense and upkeep, a burden to the owner, who, poor soul, does not know any better, until he gets aboard a vessel that does not need a cockpit. A cockpit, for mechanical and other reasons, is one of the most difficult places to keep tight in a vessel, hence the tendency for rot there. One of *Spray*'s very good points as to sea-keeping is the lack of a need for a cockpit.

I think, too, the rather high cabin trunks were of some sea-keeping use. They offered the protection a cockpit might have given without pools of water in the corners. My house also offered quite some reserve buoyancy, though it was never really called on to demonstrate this. Such a house must be of stout build—when I say sides of the *Spray*'s house were about as strong as the hull, some people look blank. I think weak deck structures are the cause of many vessels going missing. But to have very stout deck structures calls for a hull that can carry them without becoming topheavy; this the *Spray* had.

The terms seaboat, sea-keeping, and seaworthiness are all related. They are hard to define fully, and cover so many things. A book covering all aspects of these terms alone would be a very large work, and should contain a section on an aspect that is sometimes forgotten: a full belly at the right time is a part of seaworthiness; it's just as important as a good suit of sails and other sound gear. In this respect, the *Spray* model is very much suited to being seaworthy—the potential for cooking meals right is there. A banks dory adrift is quite a sea-keeper if left alone—but any unfortunate who may be adrift in her can't last too long. An open dory doesn't have a good, dry place for stores, a warm bunk, and a good stove that can work in very foul weather, but the little ship we discuss here has the potential for all of this. She has a stout build and therefore is dry below, has room for all you need, has gear both on deck and below to cope with all conditions, has tools to make repairs, and has a motion you can live with. Yes, she's a fine little sea-keeper who can hold her head up anywhere, though it's understood her skipper must have some ability and knowledge to go with her.

The *Spray*, my readers, is what I call a seaboat. Not all of her qualities come from a drawing board, by any means, or from science either; most of them were obtained by incorporating characteristics that have stood the test of time.

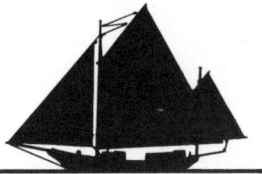

4   Above Decks

Another thing that was always of great interest to people and was much asked about was the vessel's gear on deck. Here again, it was all pretty much that of a coaster, and, seen as a whole by someone unfamiliar with it, much of its working and import was missed, or at least not understood for its true value.

Probably the most valuable bit of gear a vessel can have, especially one that is going into all sorts of out-of-the-way places, and one in which you have your all, is the ground tackle. Remember, the anchor is a symbol of Hope. Most people on viewing my ground tackle were horrified by the size of it and what seemed to them the terrific amount of "work" to handle it (the idea of work of any kind bothers many). I would explain to them that I never worried about getting an anchor up, but often did worry about getting it down in the right way, right place, and right time, as you usually have to make quick judgments, often in a strange place, to do a proper job. Think about this: you can be confronted with being under a press of sail with a strong wind, in a strange port; things you must think about are other vessels, swinging room, the character of the bottom, depth, ranges, port rules if it's a big one, and some barge in your way just as you want to luff. With experience, dealing with these factors becomes almost semi-automatic, but until you are well practiced, laying down ground tackle is one of the finer points of seamanship. Picking it up again is not that difficult.

My anchors on the *Spray* were all plain-stock, pointed-bill models of 175 and 150 pounds. I also had a 75-pound kedge. The bowers were stowed on the rail; the biggest one was to starboard as was traditional. The kedge was stowed on the cabin house. Those on the rail were hauled by a common handspike windlass and were pulled on board by an anchor purchase, which is the same as a dory tackle, a fish hook, and catheads—the easiest way to handle big anchors. The anchor cables were made up of 50 fathoms of ½-inch short-link chain, arranged so that all or part of each could be fed to either bower. The kedge had a 50-fathom manila rope that was usually stowed below. This kedge and its gear were based on about all the yawlboat could carry out in somewhat adverse conditions (this required a good yawl, which I will discuss later).

I finally wore out the big bower, as it was always put down first, so the others got little use. The soundest anchoring advice I have to give is to always use the big hook first, then you seldom need the others. I replaced the bower with a 175-pound Herreshoff pattern, which performed fairly well but which had some weaknesses. The latter I could observe in the clear waters of the West Indies. It was slow to turn over in some bottoms, and the so-called non-fouling palms did not hug the billboard on the rail. I came across a 175-pound Banks

A clear view showing the 175-pound bower stowed on the starboard rail.

A study in symmetry—the anchors stowed on the rails, with chain leading through the hawsepipes to the windlass.

anchor, the real thing, diamond-shaped wood stock and all, in fine condition—it is most unusual to find one this small. This was an ANCHOR! After a wild night on some good bottom, the windlass would almost stand the old girl on end to recover it, especially if the water was calm. This Banks anchor was lean and rangy, with very sharp bills and extremely stiff metal. When the anchor was on the bow, the stock almost touched the water. I loved this anchor, because it took hold in any sort of bottom, including rock, not that I chose rock to anchor on, but sometimes there was no other choice. The old bill-type anchors will hold most of the time on rock, even though it can wreck them—a sunken colonial fort,

Opposite: *The foredeck of the* Spray, *showing the arrangement of the windlass and the chain. This is heavy gear, but there's plenty of room to handle it.*

not marked on any chart, was the beginning of the end for my original starboard bower.

Even though I know I'm on the shelf and living in the past, my idea of security is still a rusty monster of an anchor with a long shot of oversize chain. Think of me sometime when you go adrift with modern tinware. I've used the new stuff in skippering other people's craft. I've dragged a lot, too, mostly because the ground tackle was too light and the craft were not fitted to handle anything else.

These heavy anchors were worked just as they were by any sailing vessel of the past. Nowadays, most of this is a mystery. Let's assume we're entering a port or cove. The halyards are taken off the pins and cleared for running. Possibly the topsail is taken in. Some of the anchor chain, which stows in a box on deck, is ranged ahead of the windlass barrel; the amount of chain is based on the depth of water. The palm lashing is cast off; the spade palms will keep the anchor on the rail, which is protected by metal. Extra turns are taken off the catstop, and a handspike is laid handy, usually along the windlass barrel so it won't roll. The skipper chooses his spot, the jib is hauled down, as is the spanker aft, and she's tended to a stop and then steered for sternway. With sternway on, all but a turn under the pin is cast off the catstop. The handspike is used to pry the palm off the rail, and a split second later the catstop, which has been under one's foot (the left foot if it's the starboard anchor), is let go. This tends to throw the anchor ahead of the chain in the proper position. Yes, you can throw a big anchor with its own gear, once shown how. There is the hollow rumble of the chain over the windlass barrel (along with a cloud of rust in old vessels), and in a little craft like the *Spray* you jam the handspike in the hawsepipe to check it, surging it a little to make the anchor dig in. By the way the vessel trembles when she fetches up, you know she won't drag that night.

Ready to let go the anchor. The halyards are off the pins and cleared for running.

I still delight in that hollow rumble of the chain on letting go—it's signalling that you are there, having made a passage, even if it's only across a sound. Somehow, nylon running across a chrome-plated chock in an ultra-modern craft leaves me cold—no romance in it at all. Besides, the boat the nylon's attached to often drags during the night. I fully expect, before I'm too old to get aboard, to make a cruise in a Maine dude schooner just to hear the hollow rumble again in bringing a vessel up. No doubt there will be some rust.

Now about getting the anchor on board again. This is such a horrendous idea to nearly everyone, I will tell a yarn about it first.

My last professional yachting command, a powerful schooner of the coaster type, was acting as tender to The Commodore and his racer on a well-known annual cruise. We carried spare gear and sails, fed the racing crew, and bunked some of them. After a hard day of it (for the racers, though not for the tender, except in the galley department), we were anchored in a well-known, sometimes windswept, rather deep harbor with a fresh nor'easter on. The racer was lashed alongside, we being her anchor, with plenty of fancy rubber fenders between us. After supper it was airing on, and I considered it wise to render out more chain, about 65 fathoms of ¾-inch on the 275-pound stock anchor. We lay well all night, though it was sloppy for small craft.

The next morning after the gang was fed, it was suggested that since there was plenty of manpower on board, some of the racing crew give a hand heaving in. After all, the cook faced a mound of dishes and deserved to be left out. All were willing enough except one, who whined and fussed, and accused me of paying out too much chain—beef and groan. I pointed out to him that he slept all night undisturbed and that I assumed he pumped a genoa winch all day. The Commodore, who sensed what it was all about and who was a fine gentleman of the older school, simply strolled forward and glared at his man. The windlass pawls clanked merrily.

Some people, I really believe, would sooner drive ashore than pump a windlass.

The sound of the windlass pawls always thrills me—it's the sound of getting underway, maybe to far places, adventure, what the whole thing is about. Yes, there is something very romantic about the windlass pawls' clanking.

So you get the chain up and down, wait the proper sheer, and back an after sail to give her a cast. When the hook comes away, it's best—often very necessary—to get it under foot as quickly as possible. When the anchor ring is within reach of the catstop, which should be fairly long, the stop is passed. This is easy in a small craft; you can reach it. In a big vessel, you send a man over the side. The catstop is hauled taut; in a large craft a tackle will be used. Slack the chain away, taking in on the catstop, which brings the anchor under the cathead. Snug the anchor right up; use the anchor tackle if it comes hard. Secure the anchor there and fish for the inboard fluke with the fish hook. Once the fluke is hooked, make fast the anchor burton and hoist away, bearing the anchor away from the hull—if it's a big hook, use a "spoon." Drop the anchor onto the rail, lash the fluke, and pass more turns on the catstop. Finish stowing chain (a chain hook is used to handle it) and swab down.

On small craft such as the *Spray*, all this can be done without undue strain and haste by a singlehander. I still don't recommend singlehanding as a way of life; it's just a necessity sometimes.

If any of my readers don't understand the terms used in working these anchors or can't quite picture the gear, they can find help in most of the older books on seamanship. I think anchor gear is very well shown in drawings in Howard Chapelle's book *The American Fishing Schooners* (W. W. Norton, back in print). I suggest, too, that my readers see the movie "Captains Courageous," which seems to be an ageless thing (I speak here of the movie with Spencer Tracy as Manuel, not the recent television movie). Mystic Seaport in Connecticut and similar places show it on occasion. There is an excellent, though fleeting, scene of getting an anchor aboard, casting the fish hook, the purchase, the great wooden windlass, "heaving 'round." All the flavor is there, for the movie was shot on a real schooner in action.

I've made a big thing of the anchor gear I used, with much side embellishment, I must admit. I trust by now my readers see why. No insurance company, even if you can afford the premium, no Coast Guard, no helpful neighbor, and no government weather report can give you the security of first-class ground tackle. Put real money in it—other stuff can wait. You will never regret the hollow rumble of a big anchor and chain letting go or the clanking of the windlass pawls as it comes aboard.

A steering gear and a stout rudder, even on a vessel that steers herself a lot of the time, is as important as good ground tackle. I note that many craft now are quite weak and inferior in this department. Our craft's rudder was all wood, including the stock, which is customary in this type of vessel. The hookup to the wheel was exactly the same as Slocum's in principle, though a bit more artistically put together. It was a simple drum-and-tackle arrangement. This setup was a source of great wonder and mystery to many, and they wondered why it was used. The great mystery to me is why it ever went out of use, at least in craft suited to it. Maintenance was confined to putting in a new tiller rope once in awhile and simple lubrication, all of which was easy to do because of the total accessibility to the system.

I have since used the *Spray*'s steering gear in some of my schooner designs, though usually I meet with resistance from the owners because of their lack of experience with it. It's easy to handle, quiet, and vibration-free, and you can "feel" the boat with it, if that is important to you. Besides, it's very cheap and easy to build, and therefore repair, though ours never broke down so needed no repair.

I have been shipmates with all sorts of steering gears, and on some boats the drum and tackle would not have fitted well because the boat was designed for some other arrangement. Diamond screw, R & L screw, single screw, rack and pinion—most of these were developed on the Chesapeake and are mechanical gears, some power operated. None are any better than the drum and tackle, when the latter is suited to the boat; most are not as

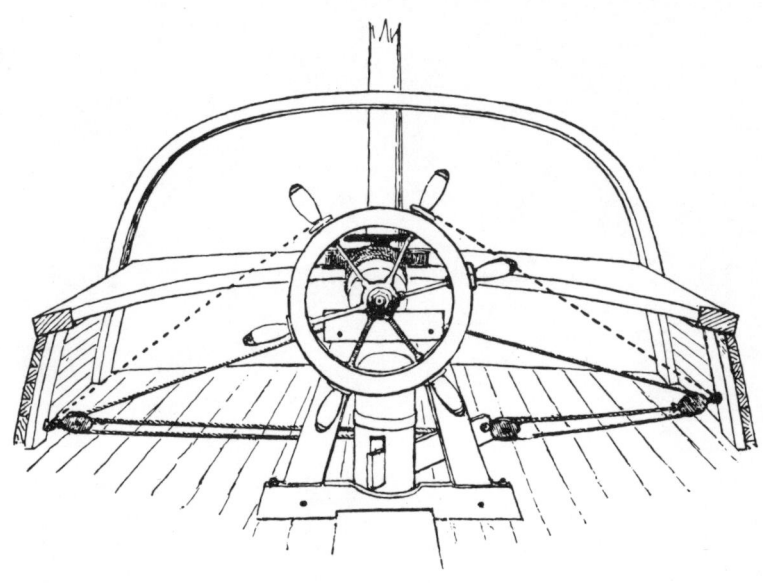

A drawing from Sailing Alone Around the World *showing Slocum's steering arrangement and the strongback that braced the mizzen mast.*

good—the power ones need much looking after, they all cost far more, and a real breakdown could be a tragedy. I have never found a regular tiller to have any advantage over a wheel, except some boats' layouts take kindly to it, and it is cheap. One now sees some ugly and too-short tillers. Even a tiller should have proper tiller ropes, and sometimes there should be a sheave in the tiller if the craft is large.

Most cruising boats can't carry a very good small boat because of space limitations. In recent years ever more boats fit into that category because the trend is to smaller and smaller, though much more complicated, cruising craft. The *Spray* could carry a fine yawlboat. She was

The Spray's steering tackle is visible aft of the wheel, running athwartships.

The yawlboat.

just under 11 feet and of the traditional shape. To hoist her up we had stern davits, which to me are the only way to carry a small boat. I try to use these on cruising boats I now design, even though I often run into much opposition from clients.

The *Spray*'s yawlboat, though old and secondhand, and much rebuilt, could live in quite rough water, carry a water barrel, and run out the kedge and cable. If things were quiet, she could carry the bower too, slung under her, warship style. Grub, ice, and passengers were her daily cargoes, and even with all of that, she was a prime sailer. She carried a standing lug rig with two deep reefs, so she could make it back to the vessel in a hard chance.

I think that it is far more important to spend your money to build a little ship that is big enough to carry a real ship's boat than to build one that is too small because you invested your money in every mechanical gadget now considered necessary. Our small boat was

The yawlboat was used for just about everything, including daysailing alongshore.

part of the family, much worked, but also much looked after. Not many nights did she lay astern on a painter; rather she was usually hoisted up, all or part way—no banging under the stern at every change of tide. With her plug out she took care of any rain, and we knew where she was. She had good oars and good gear, like the parent vessel, and for certain expeditions, an anchor and rode, water jug, various pieces of shellfishing gear, and things useful for just exploring. In the early war years she was equipped with a very small outboard, useful in commuting, but when age got the motor and we were back under sail again, it was not replaced.

Now to what most people call the real gear on deck and aloft: the rigging. The blocks were ordinary ship's blocks, with patent rollers. Some of the smaller blocks had wooden sheaves; most were rope stropped, because they were available at a very small cost, though they were of excellent construction. All the blocks were soaked in linseed oil, plus they were often lubricated. At that time, of course, most lines were manila and some were hemp.

The *Spray*'s standing rigging was galvanized steel, which was made up in the traditional manner and tarred. Rigging done this way and kept up, including periodic applications of tar, has almost unlimited life.

The simplicity of the *Spray*'s rigging makes me think about the vast number of people who want to complicate gear all out of proportion to what it's supposed to do. They are "fitting" happy—the more shackles and other bits they can use up, the better. I am astounded by the number of people who are ignorant of what gear should and can do. I meet men, supposedly sailors, who, if they give you a hand hauling a small craft up a beach, do not yet know which end of a fall to hook on to the boat, how to stopper it, or how to rig watch on watch if need be. They are pretty hot with a shackle, though, and carry a knife on their belt.

I once built an outboard tender for a man who was quite afraid his motor would jump off the transom—this *can* happen—and provision was made to prevent it, simply by boring a ¾-inch hole on each side of the wide motor pad to be used to make a lanyard fast, or a stern-line, too, for that matter. A line spliced to the motor and figure-eighted through the hole did it, simply, easily, and cheaply. But no, this was beyond comprehension. Instead, the owner got two snaphooks, the kind that tend to hang open, and taped them to a bit of line, for he couldn't splice. The tape, as usual, was mostly unravelled. In the ¾-inch hole he put a ⅜-inch bronze eyebolt. The transom was only 1¼ inches thick, so to take up the slack he used a couple of outsize washers, which were not enough—the bolt slopped around in the hole, wearing it badly, and the excess bolt stuck out astern marring anything it could reach. This was lashed up several years ago, yet I recently saw the boat with the lashup still there, doing its damage.

There was nothing more complicated on our craft than a four-sheave tackle, except one that had five, simply because it was the peak halyard, which had the only jig. Much of our gear used simply two or three sheaves and were no different in principle from tackles ashore. The anchor tackle was a burton, and a single one at that.

Chafe can be a big problem, but things were worked out over a period so there was very little. I think no accurate plan can be made in advance to prevent chafe totally, but experience with certain vessels and rigs can help at the start. There are so many variables that rules can't be put on paper. The rig has to be seen, though a look at a plan will tell some people a lot. On the *Spray* we did not go in big for baggywrinkle and other chafing gear, but used any and all of it where it was needed. Excess use of chafing gear adds to windage and has the potential to trap unwanted dampness.

We used deadeyes and lanyards, because they are practical, were cheap at the time, and are easy to maintain. You hear of the great difficulty of setting them up—not so at all, if you like and understand gear. Properly done deadeyes and lanyards don't need setting up often. Ours went five or six years at a time without attention, except for regular tarring. Tarring such rigging is essential, ritualistic, and not unpleasant.

I will discuss sails shortly but would like to mention the topsail here because of the importance of its rigging. Our topsail was a great wonder to many. It was a most

We used deadeyes and lanyards for setting up the standing rigging.

Above and opposite: *Setting and furling the topsail was simple and did not require going aloft.*

useful sail, and I wonder why so many gaff-rigged boats do without. It was most easy to set and take in; true, there was a system to it, but nothing at all complicated. The vessel was rattled down, but going aloft was not necessary to handle the topsail in such a small vessel. A system of clew lines and buntlines did it all. The sail could be handled by the wind, on either tack, or downwind. This topsail system has been standard on oysterboats for a long time; in fact much of our gear was rigged oysterboat style, which is perhaps the simplest and best style ever worked out for bulky small vessels.

I have studied in detail the methods of handling topsails on small vessels, both foreign and American. Without a doubt, the East Coast oysterboat methods are superior. To try and describe the rigging of the topsail on paper can be confusing and not quite accurate for all boats. I have shown much of the details in some of my later boat designs; even so, to get the job done correctly, I often have to take a modern rigger by the hand and show him each step, simply because he's not really interested. I feel the art of rigging today is very limited simply because most people are not interested in it. If you are going to have an economical craft that you can maintain yourself, you simply have to learn rigging and gear. If you go the manufactured, modern rigging route, that's fine, though it's likely you will become a slave to its setup—not at all good if you want to be independent and be able to manage your own affairs in far places.

By now my readers will know that I have no liking for the modern approach to rigging, at least not for leading the life we once led, or something close to it. Certainly, I hear from a lot of people who say they want to do just that.

Naturally, our spars were of wood, scraped and slushed once a year. We tarred at least yearly—parts of the gear more often—and we seemed to be always painting. Keeping everything in top shape is the least costly and by far the safest way to go. Yes, it's a lot of work, especially if you don't like work! Gear failure was rare to nonexistent with us; topping lifts and other things that could fail with quick and fatal results were inspected often and renewed if there was any doubt about their capabilities. When you stop to think about it, you are walking quite a tightrope in leading a life of this kind. Nothing can be left to chance if you can help it.

While not exactly related to gear, much effort was expended in preventing leaks, especially of fresh water, that could weaken our gear. The mainmast coat was handsome, well-fitting, and kept full of salt. The masthead had a long auger hole and tight plug; this hole was kept filled with turpentine and linseed oil, which eventually seeped down through the whole length of the stick. Drains were fitted and kept open around the trestle trees. The chores were never ending, and the vessel showed it. The *Spray* was known for the quality of her upkeep, which was absolutely necessary for us to engage in business with her.

The running rigging was shifted and renewed in a definite order, being moved to points of lesser strain as wear developed. The halyards and lifts had the top priority, and the brand-new cordage went for them first. Rope and marline were bought in coils and bulk, usually from chandlers catering to commercial craft. Some excellent buys turned up once in a while. We tended to stock ahead, having room for stores, which many craft did not have. This applied to all the other bosun's stores—buy when you find it right—paint, tar, linseed oil, or whatever you saw that might be needed in the future.

We were not always money rich, but we never lacked for ship's stores, including grub, coal, fuel, and tools to work with—this *is* the money for our kind of life. There were, of course, many others who worked this way, but we knew some craft that were always at fag ends, worn

Looking aft along the deck. Note the kedge lashed down on the cabin top.

out, unkept, unorganized. What became of them is hard to say; some went down at sea, others seemed just to fade into a marsh somewhere or become abandoned hulks up their last creeks.

But enough of that. Let's look around above deck on the *Spray* some more. She had 12-inch bulwarks and a 12-inch monkey rail 16 feet long starting at the gallows. Starting at the davits, which were elbow high, lifelines were led to the main rigging. The vessel never got underway till these lifelines were rigged. They were simply ½-inch line rigged at a comfortable hand height. I consider these lifelines some of the most important gear in the ship—cheap, and easy to rig and unrig quickly for docking. I must re-emphasize: the *Spray* never moved more than her own length away from a dock unless the lifelines were rigged.

Lifelines are by far the simplest and best safety features I know. A vessel of the classic type, as long as she has davits, gallows, or both, and no matter what her rig, can use the method we used on the *Spray* to rig them. Some schooners and ketches have thimbles in their after rigging to lead lifelines through to the fore rigging, yet I've never seen them rigged just as I rigged them. My simple lifelines were a tiny fraction of the cost of modern boat stanchions and lifelines. The modern stanchions are not only expensive, but also, if subjected to heavy use, apt to cause leaks in someone's bunk from water seeping under their bases.

To make a pen for a small child, I have even snaked lighter line around the main lifeline and through the scuppers—of course the *Spray* had the continuous scuppers to make this work. However, I do not recommend this as the best way to handle children's safety. The best way is to have an adult on watch at all times, a retrieving lanyard rigged to the child, and something worn by the child to float him—the Chinese junk dwellers use a dogfish bladder as a lifebelt; western sailors have other devices—it doesn't matter what it is as long as it works.

Let's go up forward. The bowsprit was a massive timber, 10 inches square at the knightheads, held down with a gammon iron and butted into a samson post. It was 16 feet long over-all, with 12 feet of it outboard. This bowsprit was not the bolted-on plank bowsprit seen on many boats, but the true ship style. It helped hold up the mainmast, protected the vessel's hull to a great extent from fouling by other craft, and was a delightful menace to the unwary, incompetent, and careless. Such an instrument can do quite a job on some

The bowsprit was a massive affair, with a chain bobstay. Note the gammon iron, which holds the bowsprit down.

cabin cruiser with a lot of glass house on her, one so unlucky as to drive down on you in a breeze, especially at night, which of course adds to the confusion—much crashing of glass and busting of frail woodwork, as the great half-inch chain bobstay saws at her topwork, while the anchor chain below saws at her bottom. Somehow, if the wind eases for a moment, all hands manage to pry the cruiser off and pass her astern on a line (usually your line), and she finishes the night relying on your anchor, stewing in her own glass shards. Such are the wonders of a real ship's bowsprit. I think a bigger craft that also sports a jibboom, dolphin striker, and backropes is even more delightful, and menacing.

Talk about jibbooms brings to mind the jib, which leads of course to the vital subject of sails. Sails were, and are, expensive, and they are a recurring expense at that. How long they last very much depends on how you take care of them and how much use they get. And, of course, the sail-carrying power of the vessel enters into the durability question. Naturally, in the times I speak of, we used cotton canvas, though near the end of our ownership synthetics were coming in.

Our sails were in the tradition of the craft they were on—vertical cut, often with a bight seam, roped all around, real clew irons at the throat and the clew of the mainsail, the whole works. Naturally, during the time we had our craft, we went through a number of suits of sails. A suit lasted about five years if they were in use year around—the passage north in the spring, south in the fall, and much cruising. Many times they were never off the spars from one year to the next, except when the spars were serviced and painted. The first suit was 15-ounce duck, and though good, we came to like the number canvas better, as it was not so stiff. We used number eight, though actually number ten is quite heavy enough if the panels are narrow. In later years the sails were Cuprinol-treated, a method I still very much favor and use for all my small-boat sails. The topsail was of fairly light goods.

The mainsail had more than one row of reef points, with each row of a different material—say, one of cotton, one of manila, and one of hemp. This was not a new idea by any means. This system was great at night, or day too for that matter, when you might have a willing stranger to reefing giving you a hand. Tack lashings and reef pendants were always kept rove, and the main, though big, being all inboard, with good 'jacks and a crutch, was no big matter to reef. With a trusted helmsman, reefing the main could be done in the lifts alone, though by doing it this way you are very much in the helmsman's hands.

I am well aware that people have differing outlooks on sails and the making of sails. In later years after I owned the *Spray*, I spent considerable time as a pro on racer-cruisers, using the most up to date of sails. My opinion is to leave them to those craft. For such craft as the *Spray*, do it like it was—use either cotton or flax, built like they were in the past. In my dotage, I get no pleasure at all from the looks, sound, or feel of synthetic sails. I even prefer the smell of a cotton sail. There is something about the smell of a coaster's half-mildewed old foresail that has charm. This charm is part of the reason for owning a craft like the *Spray*.

The jib was about 300 square feet, with a single reef, double sheets leading aft, and a two-part halyard with a downhaul. I consider the latter a vital bit of gear. There were lazyjacks on the jib, oyster sloop style, and of course stout footropes under the bowsprit, with stirrups on them, making the sail very easy to handle in a hard chance. Ordinarily, on coming to anchor the mate took the jib stowing entirely in her charge. She seemed to enjoy being out on the footropes. Like many women mates, she's not very big, so you can see the jib was no really heavy chore, since it was fitted with the proper gear. The mainsail was about 600 square feet and handling it was not beyond the strength of a man in his prime. The throat and peak halyards were four-part, plus there was a three-part jig on the peak. The latter was mainly used for setting up the peak with the sail drawing, as it was not needed when hoisting sail with the ship's head to the wind. It's essential that the peak be properly set for the good of the main, and also to assure a proper-setting topsail. The mainsail, which had a 26-foot-by-6-inch boom, had double wire lifts in coaster style, lazyjacks, and a four-part sheet. All this was really about as simple and easy working as you could get, considering the size of the sail.

The mizzen, sometimes called a jigger, or a spanker by the old Chesapeake watermen, was about 155 square feet. It was a standing lug, with a simple two-part sheet on an outrigger (boomkin to some) and a single two-part halyard. It was loose footed and had an outhaul for the clew. Though totally outboard, the mizzen was within very easy reach from the yawlboat in the davits. This sail was simple, easy to make and use, and close winded, as a mizzen should be. It was, I think, maybe one of the earliest forms of mizzen used on yawls, though they called them Dandys way back then in England.

All of the *Spray*'s sails had permanent gaskets for furling, and all except the mizzen were faked, not rolled. The mizzen gaskets were fast on the yard, on the main they were made up on the mainboom, schooner style. The bowsprit had a set of wood jackstays, with stops rove through holes always ready for use. After 50 years of sailing in all kinds of craft, I still fail to see why a real cruising boat usually has her sail stops kicking around some place loose, and why the reef pendants, if any, are stowed away in some locker, and why all the things long ago worked out to make a craft safe and easy-working are either unknown, ignored, or shoved under the rug.

Our craft of course had some lesser deck gear, and lesser gear aloft, too. Most of the lesser gear—boat gripes, flag halyards, lantern halyards, and many other items—are more or less commonplace. If something were a little different from the usual run, it was because it suited the situation. Many visitors, coming aboard the first time, were on the lookout for all sorts of wonder gadgets, no doubt thinking that, because we lived aboard and sailed a lot, there must be a lot of wonderful things lying around that we had developed. Actually, the opposite was true. We kept simplifying where possible, though some things couldn't be simplified any further because of the high state of their development—the actual running gear, for instance; there was little one could do to improve it.

Our equipment did undergo change and improvement for obvious reasons. I like a powerful horn; we tried a couple, including a power-operated type, and settled on a hand-operated vacuum trumpet, which gave long, loud service. We also experimented with anchor lights. Nothing could take the wind like a Dietz contractor's lantern, of which we carried two. After much experiment, I managed to rig a burner of my own make to a standard anchor light with a Fresnel lens. It was bright and totally trustworthy, the first and last I could say that about. An electric anchor light was used for awhile but given up; it's now, with a different type of bulb, a hall light in my house. Our sidelights were bigger than those the vessel was required by law to carry and were oil and electric powered. Eventually all outside electricity was given up, as we felt it was not worth the extra maintenance. We found that, with proper use and care, our oil running lights, anchor light, and overhauling light were quite good and little bother to keep up. Even with today's so-called improvements in electric gear, and somewhat higher voltages, electricity does not take to salt water. When I was a pro in other people's boats, some quite electrified, I had my fill of trying to keep up with it. The sad part was that much of the electrical equipment was not really worthwhile or useful anyhow. Knowing well the interest in electronics on boats today, I remind you that it's not cheap, either in first cost or maintenance, and it uses fuel. You decide how much it is worth.

After all that, I will concede that below decks on the *Spray*, while there were some oil lights, electric lights were the way. Yet even on these there was some maintenance. I will go into this further when we consider the *Spray*'s powerplant—something Slocum did not have.

While water containers are not part of deck gear on boats today, on the *Spray* part of our water supply was on deck in the traditional casks, and I still think such an arrangement is a good one if the vessel is big and stout

There was plenty of room on deck for people to move around and also to keep water casks and miscellaneous gear. (Photo by George Yater)

enough to handle it. In our case the water from casks could easily be run into the main tanks. The casks could be hoisted in and out of the yawlboat with the ship's gear, so watering ship in far-off places was no big problem, provided the water was good. Often the water ashore was doubtful, so it could only be obtained for washing, but a cask could be easily cleaned out for good water when it was available later on. The casks were also easy to fill by catching rainwater off the cabin top, which had a lip and scuppers designed just for this sort of thing. Rainwater is pretty flat for drinking, but it's fine for all other uses.

The *Spray*'s large decks also allowed carrying fuel drums, and gasoline at that. Nowadays this is much frowned on by insurance people, the Coast Guard, and others, yet in those days it was a common practice and accidents were rare. I suppose such methods always will be used in small craft making long hauls. In the War years, we did this on a large scale.

It seems to me that in recent years there have been more fires and explosions than in the past, for the following reasons: There are more boats now than then, and along with them more people who don't know what they are doing. Almost all engines now have push-button starting, with the button quite remote from the engine. The operator never gets near the machine to see, smell, and check it before firing it up. This is asking for trouble. Even some diesel installations I have seen can cause problems, and with remote starting, the chances of battery gas or propane going undetected are very good.

We hear dire things about the fuel situation in the future. It looks as if fuel as we saw it and used it will become a thing of the past. Can you imagine filling three 55-gallon drums and topping off the tanks below with gasoline at 10 cents a gallon? At the time of that price, there was a gas war going on along our route. Fuel bought at this price was carefully hoarded to be used in a part of the world where gas sold for the outrageous price of 27 cents a gallon! A frightful holdup, we thought. Today you will not use or handle fuel as we did; no matter, I just show how we, and many others, did it then.

There is really little more to say about ship's gear above decks, as it was all the very simplest. We did not have that sailor's curse, "Big ropes, small blocks to ya, light and variable with a rolling sea and rain!" In any case, traditional rigging is all down in books on seamanship, in many books of plans, in museums, naval history collections, and in many other sources. Those who are interested can get to it.

5 Below Decks

As navigation gear is betwixt and between—most of it used on deck, much of it stowed below—we might take it up next. I have never been greatly excited by navigation as a hobby as many are, but consider it a necessary chore that goes with sailing, to be done as simply as possible for reasonable results. We carried a small sextant of good construction, too small in some ways, but good enough for the little use we gave it. On deck in the fore rigging we kept a harbor lead always at the ready; there was also a double-ended sounding pole stowed along the rail. Both of these were most important for shoal-water work, of which we did a lot at times. We had a deep-sea lead line below; it was not often used.

The compass was an excellent seven-inch Richie, built in 1877. It had a hand-painted card, and, though it had apparently not been overhauled since it was made, it did not have a bubble. It was, and still is, my favorite compass. The card is turned up at the edges like a pie plate, so you look squarely, not at an angle, at the markings. The card is in points and quarter points—no degrees—this is all any sailing vessel needs. The compass was hung in the cabin and was viewed from on deck through a hole covered by a wood slide in the after end of the house. It was lighted by an electric rig of my own make; the backup was an oil light. Neither ever gave any trouble. The compass was most steady and easy to use. I have not found anything of later build to be as good.

We also carried a spare four-inch compass, which we used only for bearings as it had a sight ring. Much practice made it possible to use the big compass for bearings as well, in spite of its location, with very good results and with less fuss.

The big compass was not compensated, but it did have a deviation table, which really was not referred to often, because we knew the error by heart from long use. The error was not large and was "semicircular," so it posed no big problem. Various hand-bearing compasses were tried at times, and we found that all were next to worthless, except if used in awkward locations. The vessel was just filled with too many iron fastenings, rigging, and fittings for these little things to work.

Down below there was a vast chart locker, and when necessary the cabin table became the chart table. There was also a chart case that lived on deck and which was most handy for alongshore work. Though we had protractors—we found the type with a string instead of an arm was best—we usually used parallel rules. Naturally, we carried and used dividers and such gear. For inshore work I relied on sticks with various scales cut in them. During the War years, especially in very high-speed craft, I found that a round stick (untapered mop handle) with various scales cut in it was ideal as a rolling rule for fast work. In speedy craft, things jump around and you often find the usual navigation equipment absent. This very sophisticated nautical instrument stows well in a seaboot when you are living out of a seabag.

We carried other nonessential bits of gear as well as a few essential ones—a barometer, a ship's clock, and, after a couple of trials, an all-wave radio receiver designed for light aircraft. This receiver was the best I've ever used—economical of power, far reaching, and fairly noise-free. It was outstanding for its time. We had really no need of a chronometer, as time signals were readily available by radio, and where we went, this sort of thing was not often needed. We had both a taffrail log and a chip log. The mechanical log was never used in areas of much weed or where gamefish were known to feed. The chip was under these conditions more reliable, though more trouble to use. Actually, we became very expert at estimating our speed, and our results were as good as the logs or better. Staying with one craft over a long period of time and always observing makes this possible. There was a log slate just inside the companion, so the person on watch could note the time and other information. We had good luck in thick weather, with not many close calls, and we had no electronics to keep us from being in tune with our natural surroundings.

Many people have seen dummy clocks that are used for recording departure time or ETA. At one time I made up a board, using clock hands, a compass card, estimated speed, and I don't know what-all, sort of a traverse board, but I never did anything with the idea. I think someone tried manufacturing this for awhile, but it did not go over. It was just another gadget—the old slate handled it all.

Since my days on the *Spray*, I've used radar, RDF, Consolan (while it lasted), depth sounders, and of course the noise-maker ship-to-shore radio. I think the depth sounder is a true wonder, once you learn how to use it. Keep in mind it has a heeling error in a hard-pressed sailing craft; you must learn to judge this. A reminder: most RDF on small craft are not calibrated—they should be "swung" and a table made, just like a compass, otherwise they are only a guide to where the land lies. You can find the broadside of America by cheaper means.

If I have made a small thing of navigation, it's because I felt at the time, and still do for that matter, that it's a needed chore that goes with sailing. Present times are different. There are all sorts of instruments available now to those who can afford them that were not available to small vessels when we were at it. Too, traffic patterns and navigational aids have changed since our days in the *Spray*. Large craft now depend on radar and don't slow down, though the law says they should. At the speed these ships go, a human lookout (also still required), if he's on duty at all, has to sight and think faster than in the old days. Aids to navigation are more numerous and more geared to the use of electronic stuff. I mourn the passing of the lightship and its delightfully vulgar diaphone, whose unmistakable Ggrrruuummmp!! was most comforting—even when you couldn't quite hear it, you could feel it.

This talk about navigational gear has us more or less down the companionway, so we might as well look the *Spray* over below. Just how the vessel was arranged below is of no great moment, though I'll describe it as I go. I think any boat should be laid out more or less as the owner wants, so long as it's a practical setup for his use. The tried-and-true layouts work—much departure from them and unforeseen problems come up.

Most people are more interested in a cabin and how much you can jam in it than they are in the rest of the craft. Visitors to the *Spray* were avid to see below, here again expecting all sorts of trick things and folding whatnots. There were a few things below these people had never encountered before, simply because they had not seen a boat in which the items would fit. There were no gadgets in the usual sense below decks on the *Spray*.

The forecastle, because the vessel was quite full bowed, was large by any standards. For a number of years, before I found a wife, it was fitted up in a rudimentary but sufficient way, for I had not decided what I wanted to use it for. As completed, the forecastle became our quarters when we were chartering—we lived aft when not, naturally. We had two big, deep bunks, by other boats' standards, and two hanging lockers, a toilet and wash basin with curtain, a dresser, good-sized shelves, locker seats, and a vast amount of storage under these and the bunks. There was a small trunk cabin over the forecastle, giving standup headroom in a small area. There was a rolling fisherman's hatch up forward plus a big cowl ventilator and two ports.

All the ship's stores (bosun stores, that is) and all the tools were in the forecastle. I had three chests of journeyman shipwright tools, plus engine tools and repair gear of all kinds. As if this were not enough, there was an auxiliary lighting plant, switchboard, and batteries, and in the middle of it was an auxiliary engine covered by a hinged table. Also, most of our possessions, at least the wearable ones, lived in the forecastle part of the time, too.

If you think this is a lot in a small space, it was, yet when it was all properly stowed, there was much more moving-about room than in the total cabin space of some recently built cruising boats. In very hot weather, it could be hot in our forecastle, but not impossible; it was sometimes noisy, but usually it was a dry and snug retreat. We never had wet bunks and the machinery did not smell—its warm iron was more of an asset than a bother. I have spent time in many forecastles and have designed a few, yet for the size of the *Spray*, I think we had them all beat.

As I said, the quarters were our home when we were

Above: *Inside the main cabin.* Opposite: *Looking into the main cabin.*

not carrying guests, and were for their use only when we did. Starting from forward, there was a large double stateroom that extended the width of the ship, with 5 feet by 6 feet of floor space. In it were wide, deep bunks with a fantastic amount of space for canned goods under them. There were shelves of all sorts, a full-length hanging locker, with room for hats and shoes, two smaller lockers, three large ports, two ventilators, and a tiny dresser. As everywhere else in the ship, the bunks in this stateroom were recessed, and not too exposed to light, though all the cabins tended to be lighter than those in most boats. All openings were, of course, screened. Anyone who did not like this stateroom simply did not like boats! It even had a couple of chairs.

Moving aft, there was a passageway, with a toilet room to starboard, and a good one at that. This room had a locker for all the ship's linen, which was a fairly large amount because of her part-time trade. This facility, besides being roomy as these things go, was superior

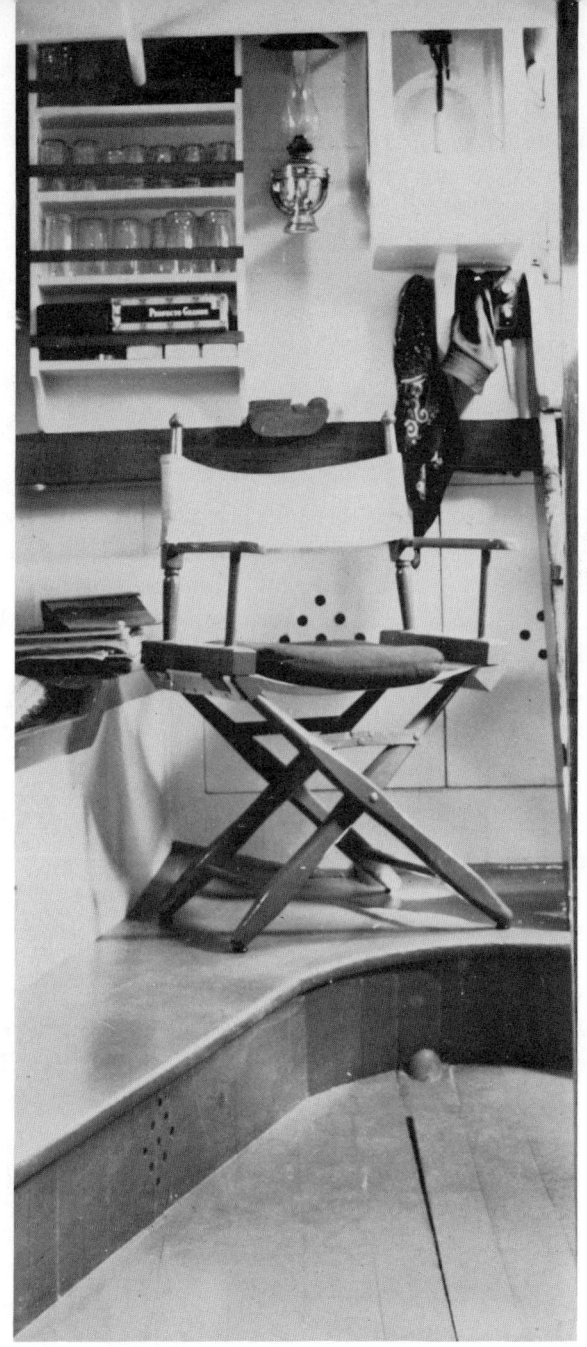

in another way—it was rigged athwartships instead of fore and aft, as most are now.

The galley, which was to port, was arranged athwartships and was more or less enclosed. It was ventilated by a big port, an overhead hatch, and a fan (not much used). The enclosed aspect of the galley did not appeal to others much, but then they did not use it, either. To the mate, who does not like to be hovered over while she's cooking, it was just the thing. I'm inclined to agree with her. The stoves were a 212 Shipmate (we had two; one wore out) and a Primus of my own design and build. I built the frame to enclose separate Primus stoves and tanks, and built an oven to fit on top. This rig rode on top of the range in warm climates, yet could be removed in minutes. The heating surface was much bigger than those on the usual stoves of this kind. The stoves and the sink were arranged athwartships, as was a nicely shaped drainboard. The top of the board had been dished out with an adz and was originally covered with zinc, which wore out. It was recovered with copper with soldered joints. I have since used stainless steel, monel, and formica for drainboards on other craft and find them all inferior to the copper, for these reasons: Copper can be dressed to pleasing and drainable shapes, while many other hard substances cannot; it takes a hot pan without the annoying humping and grunting you get with stainless steel (though this action is apparently harmless) and without the total ruin you get with formica; its surface is the least slippery—in fact, copper seems to give a slight drag to most pots and pans, enough to keep them put most of the time. Personally, I like the feel and dull, well-used look of copper.

The galley also had a small dresser that hinged down. It had a vast volume for ready stores, the usual dish and pot lockers, a vegetable bin, coal or wood box, depending on the moment, a long rack for mason jars, and a junk shelf.

I have not mentioned the icebox—it had no place in the galley. We kept two ice chests on deck, one of which was of quite good size and which was built to our own design. I believe that, if a craft has the room, up on deck is by far the best location for the icebox. We found that ice keeps much better on deck in the tropics, as at least it cools off some at night. We also found that the best way to cover these boxes in the sunlight was to use many layers of old sail folded and cut to shape. This cover, if kept wet, worked better than anything else to keep the box cool. Other advantages to the deck location of our iceboxes was that they drained directly overboard, were easy to get at, and hence were very easy to keep clean and load. One box was for the use of anyone at any time—drinks, fish temporarily, and whatnot. The bigger box was for galley use only and was in full charge of the mate—no one else could touch it. Since she made many tasty things, her orders were seldom ignored, and if by chance someone forgot, he got yelled at.

Many might think having the iceboxes on deck was an unhandy arrangement. In practice it was not at all. The smaller box was mostly used from the deck anyhow, so it saved traipsing below most of the time. A person more or less chained to a galley likes to hit the deck as much as possible, and going to the box was one more chance. Of course you darn well planned just what you needed from it, so you only opened it once for the whole meal. This is a great saving of ice when you are far from the supply. With care and planning, we could go for long spells and not run out, and if we knew we were going to run out, we planned ahead so we could simply carry on without.

Yes, we lived well, and the mate's dedication and skill

made many a roast, pie, or cake survive, when it could have been lost in a squall, tide rip, or hubbly entrance channel somewhere. I notice that weather and sea conditions have no regard for a cake that's about to rise and set itself.

So much for galleys. If a ship does not have a workable one, or has a master of it who does not know what to do, or has scant stores, she never gets far. As my long-time friend Capt. Billie used to say, "God strike the man who stints his gut to buy property!"

Aft of the galley and toilet was the main cabin, which was not at all unlike that of an oysterboat in some ways. It contained a low, semicircular seat-locker, a lower bunk to port, a Root bunk, which kids fought for, a folding bunk above it, and a chair at the after end. There was vast storage under the lower bunk and at the head of it; there was a seat with a lid to the port of the big locker, a chart locker, and a table that extended to seat six. At one end of the table was a locker for the silver, sugar bowl, salt shaker, etc. There were also book cases, the before-mentioned radio receiver, a clock, the barometer, etc. The cabin had many book shelves and pictures in frames of various kinds, the pictures being changed as the mood varied. The main cabin had two big ports, plus what I consider to be a standard companionway: 24 inches by 30 inches. The companionway ladder was a stout oak thing with wide treads.

All ports on the *Spray* had curtains to afford some privacy alongside a dock or other craft. They were simple, attractive, quickly removed, easy to wash, and always the subject of comment. The mate's invention, the curtains were simply made up with gooseneck hooks to clear the ports, which were massive, a bright piece of colored string with a button on each end, and colorful cotton dishcloths—quite cheap and expendable, yet they lasted well. Many of the niceties—little things that made living pleasant—were the result of the mate's ideas, plans, and improvements. For instance, the vegetable bin she suggested worked better than any I have seen since, though it worked nearly on the same principle as all the others. Yet things seemed to last in it.

That vegetables lasted on the *Spray* might not be totally attributable to the bin. It may well be partly because of the way the vessel was built. The *Spray* was a true wooden wall; that some called her a log cabin did not bother us at all. She was also salted between her timbers, having about a ton in her. She was dry below, quiet, and not subject to sudden temperature change—she tended to be cool in hot weather and warm in cold weather. We lived with her both in the tropics in the summer and northern climes in the winter. She was of such a shape that, as long as she was out of running ice, no amount of extreme weather had any effect on her. The *Spray* was an all-weather craft, as much as any boat can be.

The aftermost compartment in the *Spray* was the lazarette, a vast area by any standards. It had two gas tanks, a built-in ventilator, room for firewood, and—just think about this—bunker space for 1,000 pounds of coal, which she loaded more than once when the price was right. She seemed to sail better with this weight; she performed well when trimmed by the stern.

The subject of the *Spray*'s water tanks makes an interesting discussion, especially in the light of modern tank systems. Simply stated, we had a gravity system, something totally impossible to have in most craft, because they have neither the space up high to fit the tanks nor the stability to handle weight placed so high. Our tanks were right up forward, under the deck. One was forward of the massive samson post, the other was aft of it. Both tanks were heavily stanchioned and braced to the samson post and the side of the ship. The vents were internal, so there was no chance of contamination from salt water, unless we sank, in which case it would not matter. The tanks could be drawn from separately, or in unison, or they could be brought to equal levels. Each tank had its own fill pipe. The water supply to the forecastle wash basin was simply a tap off the main line, which was a one-inch-diameter galvanized pipe connected with a very tight-fitting hose as needed. At the lowest point, the main line had a tee and a pipe plug, so the whole system, including the tanks, could be drained or just blown once in a while. The main line branched into two one-half-inch lines that went to the after basin and the sink. The spigots were the nice, brass spring-loaded type, very much like those in the old-time Pullman cars.

This water system was very trouble-free. At the most, we had to blow it out once a year to clean the lines of the muddy water common to some southern ports in those days. All else we had to do was replace the washers and pack the spigots, maybe once every six or seven years. Rust was unknown to our water supply, and there was no constant tinkering with pumps, which, by the way, in late years have been of very poor quality it seems. I have never been with a more trouble-free water system since living on the *Spray*, and, as you can imagine, its original cost was modest.

While on the subject of plumbing, allow me to discuss the toilets briefly. The one in the forecastle was a commonplace model that had an intake check valve that was mechanically unsound and uncorrectable, so we simply added a hand-operated valve before it, and that took care of its failing. The after one got a lot of use, was not cheap to begin with, and was rebuilt time after time. The castings and fittings were excellent, and all the parts that wore out could be repaired or replaced right on board. We simply carried what was needed to do it. I could go on at length as to how well built this rig was, and how poorly built they are now, but won't bore my readers. The younger set won't quite believe it anyhow. To those old timers still around, who remember way back, I "Say Sands"; they will know what I mean.

The *Spray*'s fuel tanks were right aft, as far from the engine as you could get. They were made of copper and had separate fills, vents, and cutoffs. The line from each tank led to a big, very accessible filter of bronze; the main line took off from the filter and was jointless until it reached the cutoff next to the engine. This line was clipped and padded, and rode a cedar strip the whole way. It was a true gravity fuel line, since it led from the bottom of the tanks. Such a gravity system is not now approved by the Coast Guard, insurance people, and others. I still think that, properly installed, this system has merit in spite of much preaching against it. The theory against gravity feed sounds good; however, if you have a fuel-line stoppage or a fuel-pump failure with a nongravity line in a tight spot, say, with a rocky jetty close by, you "Get Religion" quick. Gravity fuel systems had to be used when engines didn't have fuel pumps in the past, and I never saw any trouble if the installation was sound. I have expounded on all this in print in other places, so I won't go into it further.

We have led fuel to the carburetor now, so there must be an engine. Actually, there was none for a year or so, then we used a motor yawlboat for auxiliary power. She was powered by a nearly unused four-horsepower, two-cycle engine that came available for a low price, so the boat was cheap and she worked well. She pushed the vessel at an even three knots in a calm, turning a 16-inch by 16-inch three-bladed wheel.

Later on, a four-cylinder inboard engine was installed in the *Spray*. It was bought secondhand and was well used. It was of a make no longer around, though once famous. The engine had a 330-inch displacement, which sounds like a big mill now, though actually it was not. It

Above and opposite: Before we installed an inboard engine, the motor yawlboat provided our power.

was just a rangy sort of beast that kept up a modest speed and was easy to live with. It had dual ignition and petcocks, and was easily hand-started. The engine turned a 22-inch by 16-inch wheel at a modest pace; its most economical gait was five knots.

The castings gave out on this engine—they were thin from age when I got it. We replaced it with a then-well-known machine of 205-inch displacement, with a 2:1 gear. The engine was installed at Ralph Wiley's yard on the Chesapeake Bay. It gave long service, though, as it

turned faster than the previous one, it was not nearly as nice to live with. It used the same wheel as the previous engine, and it turned in about the same results. Later on, we experimented with another wheel, which made little difference. It was not hard to hand-start this engine, either, but it should have had priming cocks. After a number of years, the head went, then the manifold, then the block developed an outside split. It was time to do it again.

By mail, through Wiley again, we bought another engine, a make no longer available, but one with a long, reputable past. It was also the most expensive one to be found at that time. Perhaps we were being regressive—the new one was in many ways like the first one. It had four cylinders and displaced 318 inches. It was a long, rangy, direct-drive creature that looked like an engine and was very accessible. It had petcocks and was hand-starting only, having a magneto that threw a big, vulgar spark, which could be manually set—it had to be for starting. Other features were base plates, an oil pump and strainer you could take off and have in your lap in minutes, a sight oiler on the timing gears, a water pump that never leaked, and all sorts of other wonders, or more properly the lack of them. This machine was easy to clean, quiet as engines go, vibration-free, nice sounding in the exhaust, and most economical. Compared to the previous engine, we got one-quarter of a knot more at an easy gait, on less fuel. The secret seemed to be low compression. That engine was very easy to start and always responsive.

Many people asked why the engine was installed way forward. The answer is simple—it took up the least valuable room there and was most easy to get at. Then what about so long a shaft? Heck, the longer the shaft the less trouble you have with lineup; besides, the inboard part was a big, stiff, steel thing. The engine controls also always drew comment; what a chore to take them aft. Not at all in practice. Most boats now have handrails of some sort in the cabins. Ours had one the length of the house, right down through the passageway overhead. It was simply a pipe that turned and acted as the clutch and reverse drive. Within this pipe was a smaller pipe, packed in grease; this was the throttle. These pipes connected to the engine via the forward bulkhead by levers, and led aft outside to out-of-the-way, but handy, controls near the wheel. This arrangement was cheap, efficient, and good looking, and required no upkeep or repair. We went through three engines, but the controls and shaft remained constant.

We had no gauges or instrument panels outside; the last engine had only a big oil gauge just inside the fore hatch. The engines were started from below—a system I still favor, though long out of style. I like to see, feel, and smell the engine before starting it. You are unlikely to have trouble this way. By being prudent, we never ever had even a slight suggestion of a possible fire aboard, from the machinery, stoves, or electrical system. Many cannot say as much.

I am quite sure that, with the present outlook and modern inaccessible machinery, rules, laws, and whatnot, our methods used then are outmoded and out of place. It is well to remember, however, that they worked, and very well at that. Being safe aboard ship is like handling firearms—you have to learn how. I am still not adjusted to today's concept that you must do it all the hard and expensive way, because some agency wants to protect you from yourself.

Though all of the machinery on the *Spray* used lubricating oils economically, as do marine engines, because they run at a constant, steady speed, we still had a built-in lube-oil tank. Buying in bulk saved money way back then, as lube oil could be purchased in bulk cheaply by present-day standards. Besides, we did not spare oil. Our changes were frequent, and the engines we used were 10-quart jobs, not a bit like the new mills that take a little oil, circulate it fast, and attempt to cool it by circulating water—all this requires another bit of gear and provides another chance for leaks.

We were not at all afraid of using through-hull fittings. As long as they are looked after, they are no problem. On the *Spray*, those for the engine intake were dual. The main cooling-water discharge was high up, just under the guard; you simply looked over the side to see if all was well there.

Below decks we had rather good electric lighting, though of lower voltage than that used now. With proper fittings, very big wire, and good outlet locations, our system did better than some that were more complicated, though not as well worked out. Our system underwent change and improvement over a long period. We had some current-saving ideas that worked well, based on the equipment that could be obtained at the time, and were used when a very small amount of light was needed, say, underway at night, when reading in a bunk, or when there was a gang aboard just having a gam.

To feed this system of lights, every engine we ever had, even though it might have a generator of its own built on for starting, worked a belt-driven generator to tend the lighting system. The generators could be crossed to either a starting battery or a lighting battery in case of some failure, though generally each tended only to the job it was laid out for. The last engine, which had no starter, pulled two generators, so in effect we kept the original dual system. Both the standby battery and the starting battery were the usual lead-acid type.

The main lighting battery was an Edison nickel-iron, soda battery, and to my way of thinking the best and most durable lighting battery ever made. It was not designed to start engines, and its charging characteristics were different from those for lead batteries. To charge this main lighting battery, we simply had an auxiliary independent generator of our own assembly. This was just a Briggs & Stratton engine that was belted to a heavy-duty generator, which allowed a great amount of amperage variation. The generator was also wired so it could handle either battery. By changing the belt, the Briggs & Stratton could also run a gear pump that could clear the bilge—a standby that never saw use. The switchboard was designed to handle the above system.

Except in cases of emergency, the lighting system had what is called a floating ground. People have been arguing the pros and cons of this grounding method for years. All I can say is that we never had any electrolysis, and an electrical failure below decks was rare.

Now hear this: our engines, all of them, did not have pans under them, yet the bilge never had any oil in it. At least while we owned the vessel, the brass-barrel bilge pump aft near the steerage always discharged on deck—proof of our confidence that the engines would not leak oil. This may be possible today, but it is most unlikely. Today's modern machines turn fast, work near the top of their ability, are installed in inaccessible places, and use extra piping and joints—all likely to cause oil leaks. On the *Spray*, we did not work our machinery hard, except when we were in a cramp of some kind. We found the vessel's gait, where the auxiliary engine seemed happy and the fuel use was reasonable, and ran her that way. I estimate we used about 15 actual horsepower most of the time, maybe less.

Of course, in those days our auxiliary engine was saltwater cooled, and the engine was built for it. The exhaust system, too, was built to temper the high maintenance common to that part of an engine's gear. Even so, we went through two of them. Our exhaust line was made up of large, hard-drawn copper tubing and was quite long, as the exhaust exited at the stern. The curves in the line were gentle, and those joints steep enough were brazed; the others were simply made up of hose. Part of the cooling water went in the exhaust line, of course, and the system required no muffler because of its length. The measured beat of the exhaust was not at all unpleasant, and of a kind you no longer hear, though in those days it was not uncommon in large schooner yachts whose installations were much like ours.

Looking back on it, we may have been, by present boating standards, sort of primitive, yet on reconsidering, especially after looking at some of the so-called up-to-date craft, we may have been very far advanced. We were about as self-contained as you could get and still lived in quite some comfort, not to say style, even though it was only a style of our own. Certainly our craft and her parts were far more accessible for routine upkeep and simple, or even major, repair than they seem to be now. As you might gather, at one time I did a lot of tinkering with machinery, and to an extent still like to. But due to stiffening joints, trifocals, and maybe just a cussed outlook on the modern scene, I don't care at all to work on the ultramodern marine engine, big outboard, or today's auto. They are all based on the same thinking—mass produce, don't repair in the old sense, simply take it out and send it to the reconditioning plant, buy new parts, and make the parts unreachable without tools designed for them. As one of my friends says, all machinery today is designed by sadists.

6   Upkeep

To maintain a vessel like the *Spray*, or any other for that matter, you must be willing to work and to maintain some sort of order, based on the seasons and how and where you use the vessel. Bottom work, especially if the boat is sailed in the tropics for some period of time, is most necessary for the good of the vessel and peace of mind. A craft is only as good as the condition of her bottom.

We did our hauling out in country yards in the Chesapeake Bay as much as possible. We used several different yards at different times, depending on who had a clear railway when we showed up. We often waited some time for a turn, which we didn't mind, since the country is most pleasant to do other chores in. And, of course, there were friends to visit. Small yards in those days were often so short on help they were happy to have the boatowner pitch in and get the job along, so they could haul another boat. Fouling is very bad at times in the

South, so we used the same system in smaller Florida yards. Besides protection from worms, a clean, well-painted bottom adds so much to good sailing and fuel economy. No one really likes bottom work; the ship is out of her element and dirt gets tracked aboard, and there are other inconveniences, but it's a necessary evil.

Sometimes, when there was a slack, we ganged up with several other small craft to be hauled at once on a 1,200-ton railway that catered to big craft. Six of us coming out at once made it worthwhile to lower the old monster down, and the rate divided among all the boats was very cheap. And in a big yard like that we were all washed off at once with a very powerful ship hose. If underwater work was required, the workmen were skillful and fast, no matter what the job—replace a plank, caulk, or machine and install a new shaft.

Most often we got our bottom paint at these yards, though we also carried our own stock in case some small yard found itself running low. Though we always used the ordinary commercial copper boat paints, we did find a couple of brands that seemed to work better in some waters. One well-known brand made in New England was a favorite with us in the South; even most of the shrimp boats there favored it, too. Strangely, this paint did not do so well, for us at least, in northern waters— we used another brand there. You learn many strange, unexplainable things when you live aboard for long periods.

By my own standards, if not by some other people's, the *Spray* was very well built. Other than routine scrubbing, scraping at times, and painting, the only other underwater work to amount to anything while we had her was to make back the seams and repay them at the boat's age of 15 and to replace part of the stern tube— the vessel had no shaft log in the true sense. I remember she needed a new pin in the lower bobstay, and occa-

Left: *Hauled out on a small railway in a country yard.*

We concentrated on the underwater hull during haulout time. This photograph gives a clear view of the Spray's *stern gear.*

sionally a renewed rubber stern bearing. We learned some things here, too. Once when rubber stern bearings were in short supply and we couldn't find a replacement, we had to turn over the one in use; these bearings wear down and to one side due to shaft rotation. To our surprise, the turned-over bearing ran like new, so, after making a device to pull these bearings without damage, we always turned a bearing over before replacing it. Our modest shaft speed may have had something to do with our success. Various experts told us this would not work, but it did, and we never had to replace the shaft, which showed very little wear.

We replaced the worm shoe at times, especially the after end, which is sacrificial anyhow. We took particular care of the massive rudder, and unshipped it at each haul to copper the port and stock, and to check the backing chain and other fittings. After 23 years, the rudder gudgeons and pintles showed remarkably little wear, due to their design. Backing chains wear fast, as they are in constant motion underway, yet they are short, cheap, and easy to replace. I believe they lengthen the life of a rudder and its gear.

We sometimes did our topside work when we were hauled out; at other times we did it when afloat in a quiet hole. It was a matter of time, place, and convenience in a craft like the *Spray*, as the topsides were all reachable from a skiff. We seemed to be always painting somewhere and were frequently touching up, for keeping a smart craft is good business as well as common sense. The paint was burned off the *Spray* what amounted to twice all over while we owned her—not all at one time, but when and where it was most needed; outboard one year, parts inboard another, the houses another. You need dry weather to burn paint and you must start early, for the wind usually comes up later. We never did more in a day than could be properly sanded and primed before dew fell. We used an ordinary quart-size gasoline blow torch, the kind you seldom see now.

I note that burning off seems to have gone out of favor in most boatyards now, for several very good reasons and some not-so-good reasons. Instead, gallons of not-cheap paint remover are used. Under the right conditions and locations, I favor burning, as it dries and hardens the wood, which makes sanding afterwards very easy. I think, too, that our way was the most economical.

As boats go, ours was extraordinarily tight in the decks, yet the main chore there, and in any craft, was the constant guard against and the repair of any leaks that developed. You do get deck leaks at times in spite of everything, and the thing to do is to fix them immediately. After all, if you live aboard, it is likely that you have all your possessions under those decks. If you can prevent fresh-water leaks, a craft will have almost an endless life, perils of the sea excepted. A leak unnoticed for even just a couple of weeks, in the right place and temperature, can cause decay, which never seems to atrophy but rather spreads.

It's said a new vessel that can get by seven years with little or no decay, assuming she's kept up, will last a long time. If, in this period, any decay is found, it should be drastically cut out. I suppose the *Spray* did as well or better than many. She had a plank go bad between wind and water in spite of being salted. We also had to replace a small part of a waterway, one hatch runner, and a place in the stern, the latter a time-consuming repair, as it was done under adverse conditions. The first mainmast, though seemingly a nice stick, did not last long. It went bad right in the clear, halfway up. The second mainmast, a hard, heavy old timer out of another vessel, seemed capable of going on forever. It was stiff, took a lot of chafe, and was tough to scrape, but looked very nice when clean. As mentioned before, we slushed the masts; the booms and the gaffs, which never gave any trouble, were painted. Slushed masts make an easy-working ship, protect the sticks from chafe, and are a cheap way to go. There was no varnish to maintain at all outside, though it was used considerably below.

As much as possible the vessel was wet down morning and evening—washed down, I should say—with salt water, and this of course is what kept her topsides in excellent condition. That this is no longer the custom of most yachts is the reason why there is so much leaking topwork and decay. Most of today's craft are so built that they take much water below if you wash them down with much abandon, anyhow.

Our topmast was often housed for maintenance; this was a small operation: slack up the topmast standing rigging and flag halyard, reeve the heel rope (a dumb sheave in the lower part, the doubling, was provided for it), take a strain, sometimes bumping the heel of mast with a maul, take out the fid, and lower it down to the cap. When the mast was down, we checked the head and fittings, painted the portion finished that way, and then sent the mast aloft a short bit at a time, scraping and slushing as it went. We did, on rare occasions, house the topmast to pass under some bridges; the vessel had a height of about 56 feet from the water to the top of the wind pennant staff. Housing the topmast under those circumstances was no big thing to do.

Not a long time back I saw a new, large schooner built for the tourist trade, and her topmasts could not be housed. I was told this was the result of some notion of the Coast Guard, or perhaps some other misinformed outfit. However it came about, masting a craft this way is a fine example of bureaucratic stupidity, ignorance of the sea, and overall lack of knowledge on the part of someone or many. I never really understood who was responsible; I therefore don't know just who I am condemning, but if the shoe fits, wear it!

The point is, any rig should be flexible and capable of easy adjustment and repair. I much prefer a separate topmast, if one is needed, to having a mast and topmast all in one stick. A broken topmast that is a separate entity will not cripple a vessel, which was very much part of the thinking aboard our craft. If something went wrong, there was a simple way out and the problem could be easily repaired. As it worked out, on board the *Spray* there was very little that went wrong.

I have mentioned painting more than once. Actually painting was rather routine; we painted when it was needed and we had a chance to do it. Above water we used nothing but good-grade oil paints, those referred to by some as house paint. I have been sternly lectured about the fallacy of using this type of paint by more than one expert and have always had the fun of saying that I had been using it for 20 years on the same craft, and that no doubt they were right, but I was going to experiment just a few more years to be sure!

Good maintenance, no matter what materials are used, is a matter of keeping at it, when conditions allow and as soon as possible. I can think of nothing better to prevent trouble and keep the vessel ready at all times. When you are cruising, you often find you are forced into taking a chance of some kind due to rapidly changing circumstances. A vessel and gear that are in fine condition usually bring you through, even when they are subjected to some sudden, unusual strains. You can maneuver with peace of mind, because you know things are right.

As I mentioned previously, on the *Spray* we had a full set of journeyman ship carpenter tools, three chests. Most of these tools were not needed for work on board, though in theory we were quite well equipped for major repairs, such as making a mast, replacing a plank, rebuilding a cabin house, or changing the interior below. There were enough engine tools to do a valve and ring job right in place, and to raise the engine to drop the pan. In fact we could and did take an engine out and replace it with another with the ship's gear.

The cabin house was, with the addition of a couple of two-inch planks to take the chafe, an excellent workbench. We built a couple of panel doors there, and no end of other things. We had tools for soldering quite heavy stuff, relying on the gasoline torch for heat, though a Primus stove did as well. Sometimes a soldering job was big enough so that both were employed. We did a lot of repairs that others said couldn't be done.

We were quite well equipped for electrical work, at least enough for our simple plant. Somehow, every craft of no matter what size or era that had electricity required much maintenance. This was not always difficult, but constant tinkering was required to keep it all working. Today, with much more electronics and perhaps better fittings, the ratio of tinkering time to amount of gear still seems the same or more.

Like a lot of our other work, engine overhaul was periodic. There was no waiting for things to fail. The need of a valve job gives ample warning, as do many other motor ills. If you do much shoalwater work in the South, no matter if you are fresh- or salt-water cooled, there will be sand and sludge to remove often. We ran the same packing in the inboard stuffing box for 15 years, simply because there was a grease cup right on the box and it was turned down at regular intervals when we were under power. Another thing that preserved the packing was that the two-part shaft had been excellently machined, something you don't always find today, and I will tell you why—it's because of either ignorance or of cutting corners to save costs in machining, something you pay for later.

A propeller shaft must have centers established at each end to be machined. Most shafts have a coupling on one end; our shaft, with an inner stub shaft of steel, had a coupling on each end—these were the common cylinder or straight-bore types, with the usual centering steps. The couplings were a slight heat-fit to the shafts; in other words, you had to expand them a bit to tap them on. The keyways were accurately handcut by a country machinist in a way few know how to do them now. The shafts were spot bored for set screws, two to a coupling, with lock nuts, and bored and wired besides. No amount of tightening the set screws could cock the couplings on the shaft—they fit too well. The keys fit the keyways with a tap fit and were left shoal enough on top not to jam the coupling outward. When all this was fitted up, the shafts with the couplings on were put back in the lathe between centers, and the faces of the couplings were "wiped" with the lathe tool. It usually did not require much. A shaft machined like that will run true forever, unless it gets bent. That is why our shaft and packing were trouble-free.

Our stoves, especially the Primus stoves, got hard use. All stoves require maintenance, and we had laid by, over a period, quite a collection of burner and pump parts. Releathering fuel pumps was commonplace, as was replacing burner needles and valve packing. The burners themselves get thin in time, so we would replace the whole unit. The tanks gave little trouble. As mentioned previously, the coal range wore out; that is, it burned out. But other than total replacement, the stove needed little, if any, repair, except a new stack and pipe fairly often. Salt and coal or wood gas seem quite corrosive to pipes, but they were then cheap and easily available, and we made our own smokeheads.

We made or repaired a lot of little things as needed, sometimes when wind bound, waiting a chance along. For instance, we built ice chests as we needed them or when we wished a change of type or shape.

The yawlboat came in for her share of repair work. She was of excellent model, though no longer young—she was built around 1913. Her keel and garboards were replaced, as were a number of frames over a period of time. A heavy repair job on the *Spray*'s stern, with no work punt handy, was done from the yawl, which was again beginning to feel her years. This job was too much for her, and she was a shaking wreck, so she was rebuilt again. Soon she was her tight and smart-sailing self again.

We did many things, repair to new construction and

back again—re-hooping a water cask, doing much sheet-metal work, making a glass-bottom bucket, building boarding and swimming ladders, doing rope work of all kinds, and making all sorts of fenders of all sizes. For instance, out of smaller, used shroud-laid line, we cable-laid a fender for the yawl, right on board. It wore and lasted better than anything on her before. We did not make sails, but we did all the repair work on them and recut a topsail we were not happy with.

Usually, at each fitting-out period, besides routine and minor things to attend to, we had some larger project that had come due—a burn-off job, deck overhaul, windlass to rebuild, or some such thing. There was stuff below to replace because it just plain wore out. In those days the vessel got plenty of use. Charter work, even with the best of clients, increases your maintenance chores. If it sounds as if we worked hard at times, we did, very hard, but there were intervals of much relaxation and ease, which, as far as I can see, having worked at something all my life, is what it's all about. Work as much as possible at something you like, even if you like it only a little, and enjoy the slack times for what they are worth. I, at least, can't imagine a life of total loafing.

We really enjoyed keeping a taut ship, partly for the pride of it, but mostly because we knew that if we kept her up, she would not let us down. She was always ready and willing, and more than once seemed to say, "Stick with me and I'll see you through."

A really good vessel asks that you give her a lot; she then pays you back in more than you can ever give. Some say certain craft exude personality and think vessels have souls. If this is so, our *Spray* was loaded with soul.

Living on Board   7

Living on board as a way of life intrigues many. Many have done it and do it now. I'll tell how we did it for the benefit of those who hope to live aboard in the future. Perhaps a description of our experiences will be of help.

The thing that made living aboard the *Spray* special was that she was comfortable, in room obviously, but great room is not all of it. Room does offer better distance between people, but two people who live on a boat, no matter how spacious it is, must think much of each other. There are times when you need a cabin by yourself, with a book or just your thoughts. A great amount of room is fine, but in some cases you can have too much. I think the *Spray*'s thick skin, steady ways, resistance to heat and cold, and easy motion were as much a part of her comfort as a lot of cabin room. Light and air, heating when needed, some degree of escape from the heat in the tropics (good awnings), ventilation both for the good of the crew and the hull, and many other little things already touched on (such as good ground tackle), make a boat like the *Spray* most suited to a floating home.

Peace of mind is important. If you don't have peace of mind, afloat or ashore, something is not right. Self-sufficiency, whether you engage in it to the limit or not, is very comforting. For one thing, you make many friends that you would not if living otherwise. I don't know if this is a bonus or not, but at least the self-sufficient friends we had were interesting. Many of my shore neighbors are not.

When we lived aboard, we seemed to have better health than many other people. Sure, we had some problems and scares, but I would say we had less than usual.

We both like to eat, and while afloat we did not spare the grub. The mate is an excellent and critical shopper. In season, when we were on the move, we had a chance to obtain things you can't get at any price staying in one place: shrimp, oysters, fish—caught 15 minutes ago—lobster or crawfish right out of the trap, fruit that falls at your feet. Having had bananas ripe off the tree, I say that what we get in the north is about like putty. Yes, I suppose you can get most of those things if you want to pay, but they have usually been too long in transit and have lost their goodness.

The variation in our life aboard was not just in food either. Sights, sounds, and smells vary in many parts of the coast. The sound and smell of the surf on a rocky northern coast is entirely different from what we find in the tropics. Even the wind sounds different in different latitudes, and you just don't get tradewind clouds where there are no trades. You might get something similar once in a while, but it's not the real thing. Endless variation and much more is one part of living aboard and cruising for fun and, of necessity, some profit. In the

Anchored in Hurricane Harbor, Key Biscayne, Florida. (Photo by George Yater.)

*Tied up at a boatyard in Fort Lauderdale, Florida.
(Photo by George Yater)*

height of your experience somewhere, you look forward to going somewhere else—it does not matter much where. There are even times, from necessity, when you are bound to a particular port to make a living, make major repairs, or settle some illness. These things usually pass, and you are glad to get going again on the vagabond life.

Making a living afloat while getting in all the sailing you want might have to be done somewhat differently now than when we did it. I won't tell you how to do it now; I will simply tell you how we did it then.

I had a trade—boatbuilding—and was able to make out at several related ones. The era we lived in made it so I never lacked work if I needed it. Working in a shipyard, painting, sailing on other craft for a while if need be—I would and could do anything. The main thing was that I was willing to go where the work was. As things turned out, there was always enough work so I did not have to stay in a location I did not like. However, this type of work, while very helpful when needed, did not give us much sailing except when we were changing sites.

Chartering seemed to be the answer. As previously mentioned, chartering was around, during my early efforts at it, though it was not as common or organized as it is now. I was single when I began. After learning the ropes a bit, I discovered that my clients were, in many cases, former owners of yachts, some of fair-size craft. The Depression had made them lay up or sell their large craft. For the most part, these people were my best clients, because they had a good understanding of what sailing is all about. We had some happy cruising, and I made many good friends, some with a name in boating in those days.

Having broken in on my own in chartering on the Chesapeake and having become mildly successful, at least in that area, I thought it was time to hit the bigger time, so I gave the *Spray* a thorough winter refit, did a lot of paperwork, and one spring I headed for Long Island Sound, with a full booking made during the winter (I could not very well miss with any luck). I set up base at a then-famous yachting center, known for its shipyards, at the western end of the Sound. Without really thinking about it, I was coppering my bets, with yards under my lee in case chartering went soft.

I had friends a little farther along the Sound, former clients and others, but I was made welcome where I was based. There were good services offered at a good price. Still, I was looked on as a yokel from the South, with a most unstylish craft. Agents of all sorts wanted to tout the vessel, for a percentage of course. They could not imagine that I was fully booked for a long season when I arrived. Once they fathomed that, they thought after one season I would learn city methods and be smoked out.

Instead, I had all sorts of luck—no breakdowns (the winter refit paid off), I met my wife (she was part of a charter party), managed to book a southern trip, and fought it out with the 1938 hurricane. We won the battle with the hurricane. Neither we nor the party I had on board received a scratch, though men and ships were falling all around us. All hands did their part, and the great ground tackle did its stuff right to the bitter end. Though we had many close shaves, no other craft hit us. The vessel jumped and shook at times like a hooked bluefish. When the storm finally let go, we all felt, along with being most thankful, that we had been in a giant washing machine—the thick coat of tar on the fore side of the vessel's rigging was gone. I had been in a couple of hurricanes before, and was sunk in one years later (in another craft), but I've never felt wind blasts like those in that one. Sometimes the craft seemed to lift right out of the water; at other times she felt as if she was sinking

The mate.

in beer foam right up to the house top. Oh! she fought back, her great iron claws hooked in. That took place a long time ago, but I love her for it still.

I took on a permanent mate that fall; she quickly became a fine cook, seaman, and helmsman. We had a nice cruise south (with paying guests partway), a profitable winter, and visited many places. Then we moved north to refit in the Chesapeake. We preferred the Bay, both for the pleasure of the area and for financial reasons. As we were well booked ahead again for Long Island Sound, we based at the same west-end port. Even though it had drawbacks, it was handy in some ways and we had made more friends there.

It soon became apparent, however, that we were being blackballed in a quiet way. We were successful while other craft lay idle, and we did it without the benefit of the Establishment, except its purveyors of supplies and services, which we paid well for. Pressures were brought to bear, so that things supplied became poor and in one case nonexistent. Some of our friends in that port were in the business of supply and were sheepish about what was happening, but they felt pressures from above somewhere. We were gone so much it was no big matter, only irritating, and it was soon noticeable to the blackballers that when we did come in, we took on less fuel than usual, little or no canned stores, and precious few other things we could manage to handle elsewhere, even though we were busy to the point of exhaustion sometimes.

What a paradox. Those craft lying idle, working under the local thinking, were not buying any stores, and many owed money. We paid cash at once. Truly, some birds foul their own nests.

Fall came again and we were off to other cruising grounds. We had no problems like that in the South in those days. We were all very happy, and grub was mighty cheap, if different, there. Imagine fine Georgia-made country bacon, two pounds for a quarter; very large ice cream sodas for a dime; or the Saturday night special of two sodas for sixteen cents—give your girl a treat!

Getting through the East River again come spring, we had a fair wind and went by our former base of operations with a broad wake. I might add that there is indeed justice in this world. The west-end port boomed during the War like everywhere else, but then fell into decay. I visited the place years later on other business and found it a hollow shell, with even some of the shell caving in.

We based at a very-well-known port farther along east thereafter, a port known for some big-time yachting scenes in the past and now. We based there until we gave up cruising and went ashore. We were there both before and after the hostilities. The years we were away on account of the war made no difference to our suppliers. Heck, they acted as if we had only been away a week—no emotion, the same reserved, friendly manner, everything just as it was, except the bulldog, who in five years had become fat and wheezy.

Much later on, I was a professional for a number of years on a yacht owned in that port and dealt with all these old friends. It was always the same—a good port and good people, and we all profited by it. Though my cruising now is all landbound, I still like to visit this place once in a while just to browse around.

I tell these yarns just to point out that receptions vary from port to port if you charter. People are people, that's all. Much later on we were beginning to be pressured a bit in our southern haunts, or at least we were getting warnings. At that point it did not matter. Subtle pressures, other signs on the horizon, and some things to come only guessed at made us consider the shore life we knew must come. In fact, on our last run to the South, we ignored work and took the winter for our pleasure—that is, no charters, though I did help out a long-time friend in a boatyard over his rush period, as he had come to expect. He saved certain jobs for me.

When you are living aboard, there can come a time of world strife or other unavoidable upheaval. What to do?

Wintering over in the South.

Some of our compatriots stuck to their way of life, though a lot gave up and went back to living in a more acceptable (to most people) manner. Among others, we stayed with it and laid up the *Spray* during World War II in a southern town in a snug canal. In fact, seeing the war clouds forming, we planned it that way.

At first I worked in the shipyards and commuted to them by skiff; as fortune would have it, housing ashore became scarce, expensive, and crowded. On the *Spray*, though she was laid up, we were in an excellent position. We were on our own, the dock rent was tiny, we were clear of the mob and in a relatively cool spot for a southern port. The vessel had all her gear sent down and stowed, she was covered all over with awnings and skirts on the sunny side, and the decks had canvas runners—in fact she looked about like an old-time warship laid up. We had fresh water at the dockside, and filled the tanks weekly whether they needed filling or not. The mechanical systems were run occasionally, though they did not do any work, and the electrical system was isolated from the running lights and was replaced by shore current. Though the shipyard hours were long and we always put in a six-day week (in emergencies, seven), there was time for some maintenance and a few social pleasures, usually among our own kind. We were faring pretty well as a ship and crew.

We built so many ships up, down, and around the coasts that Uncle Sam started looking for crews to man them. Many of us signed up and, either by chance or wise government policy, most of us manned boats like those we had been building, which meant we understood them and had few problems handling them. This left the mate alone as shipkeeper, along with three or four others in the same fix nearby. For her, it was a lonely existence most of the time, and all the upkeep fell on her. She did an excellent, dedicated, and what must have seemed at times an unrewarding job, with no end in sight. Others in the same situation did not do nearly as well. Many of the little ships went almost to pieces from neglect, and there was internal strife, causing eventual loss of a way of life once much sought after.

When I was away at sea during the war, there were occasional leaves, though for a while they were impossible to come by. When leave did become available, it usually involved much travel of an unhandy sort, but it was still much looked forward to. Much later on, it was possible by going through much red tape to move our home to a creek near the port I operated out of. A couple of others made the move, since they were stationed at the same port. As I said, we always kept the machinery at the near ready, so once permission was granted to move and the fuel was allocated, we simply gathered up the skirts, unplugged, fired up, and took off on an inside passage. We ran under power only, as it was the calm, hot period and time was limited. Though our new berth was not as nice as before, its location made getting home much simpler when the chance came.

Finally, the war was about over, and my assignments became short and sometimes foolish—the military always hates to disband. At the very windup, having made somewhat of a name by getting things done, I was given a plum assignment. I became the night skipper (my own choice) of a huge G.I. ship basin, though all the craft in it were less than 200 feet. There was a very big, ever-changing fleet. I stood a double watch with a chief engineer, so we had three days off at a time. This gave us both time to do things in preparation for discharge. I worked on the vessel; the chief laid in the then-difficult-to-find stores and tools for his newly acquired farm farther south.

So we weathered it with much luck and some breaks, many of the latter made by our own efforts. We were fed up by this time with hot climates; most of my assignments had been in the tropics, too. So we rigged up and headed for the Chesapeake in the fall, the very best time to be there. We wanted to do some things we had been longing to do, and we selected a snug winter berth in a familiar creek among old friends and settled down to a thorough refit in preparation for a resumption of the old life.

Oh, it was fun to fit out again. Others around us were doing the same thing. It was a pleasure to buy coal, have canned goods and meat again, and have social evenings on various live-aboard craft, each one giving at least one fancy dinner party that winter. Actually, these parties really were well strung out over a period, as no craft could handle all the people involved at once. I can tell you there was some very fancy cooking and baking

Wintering over in the Chesapeake.

going on. Preparations started at an early hour and went on all day.

There in our creek we had some good snows; how we enjoyed them after our long tropical bout. We hauled groceries by sled and slid on the hill nearby. The creek had six inches of ice. Christmas was quite an affair in this little haven. People were happy and looked forward to sailing come spring. I think these were the happiest times most of us were exposed to for some years. They were especially sweet since we were nearly all connected with some phase of boats during the war years.

Some smart people who had never lived aboard before, having recently been exposed to the sea while in the service, quickly bought up craft that had seen much neglect and were busy restoring them. Few craft at this time were in first-class shape, and the market for them soon boomed. I could see the old pattern taking form again—call of the sea, working at a trade, boatyards becoming suddenly busy with civilian work, some recently acquired run-down craft being put back, maybe a fairly new wife, making a home afloat. We received many a visit from these newcomers. They wanted to see how we did it, as we were considered seasoned hands.

Spring came and it was time to sail and to work again, for there had been all outgo and no income all winter. It was wonderful again to have all in order, the old order. Five years had caused changes, in ourselves, in conditions generally, and in places we had been very familiar with in the past. Yet the *Spray* was the same, as was the sea, naturally; so too were the strong fair winds, the bulging topsail, the lilting gait the *Spray* had when she was going places, the song from the sink drains at speed, and the familiar lights and buoys showing bright again. Yes, it had been worth the trouble to keep everything together for another fling at life afloat, even though we knew well it could not go on forever. The vessel was still quite sound, as was all her gear, and she had new sails. We were older but still fit. The only changes were that the times were perhaps more stressful, and there seemed to be more pressures to making a living.

As before the war, we chartered, but we had other ways of earning income as well. One method was to carry cargo. Of course, a vessel must be suited to it; *Spray* very much was. She was just under 15 tons gross, which gave her certain advantages over craft that measured more than 15 tons. She had a blue document, instead of the yacht's pink one, so she could engage in trade. Because of her document, the *Spray* was easy to clear and enter in foreign ports, but she never engaged in anything other than "clearing in ballast," with all hands as crew members, which was quite legal. Once a year on

Ashore in Hyannis for provisions.

going south, as long as she did that run, the *Spray* traded coastwise, "lumber for a southern port," that is, she took a couple of thousand feet of boat cedar on deck to the little boatyard mentioned previously. This was a favor in a way, though it paid our running expenses, too. It was fun, a shock to many, and hurt the vessel not at all; the wood smelled wonderful, and in some ways, even though you had to climb around on it, was less bother than some clients. Plus the mate did not have to cook for it.

The procedure was this: We would call ahead to a little mill in North Carolina, to tell them about what we needed and to find out if it was on hand. The stock always was available, since the mill was a bigger operation than it seemed. On arrival, we loaded at the town landing at the foot of the main street; that was what it was for. The cedar, 16 to 24 feet in length, came on a truck, cash was paid, the lumber was dumped off, I loaded and lashed, and on the first fair wind we took off. On arrival at the little yard, the cedar was at once unloaded by me and the two somewhat-backward yard boys, noisily prodded by their father. Cash was immediately paid. The arrival of the *Spray* and the cedar was always an occasion.

The business setup was simple. No matter what the purchase price at the mill, the markup, long ago agreed on, was always in proportion to the price paid. Our expenses were taken care of, and the yard obtained cedar at half what it could be otherwise bought for. Everybody was happy, except the yard boys, who got bellowed at some more as they stowed the cedar in the shed. This trade continued during all the years we went south. The cedar was excellent at first. After the war it was not so good and, of course, it was more expensive. I would now consider the worst of it fine stuff and dirt cheap at the last price I paid for it.

Carrying a deck cargo of cedar for a southern port.

I know of no other craft that traded the way the *Spray* did or even something similar, at that time or since. Most pleasure craft are just not shaped for it.

We did a lot of photo work on board, including developing and printing. A number of other people who lived afloat did too, though we never more than paid expenses with it then. Some of our pictures are reproduced in this book. They are showing age but are still in good condition, even though they are for the most part products of the galley darkroom.

We did a little writing, but we really were not interested in it then. Others we knew did a lot of writing, and some were quite successful in a small way, which was sufficient for their needs. Some had jobs "uptown," usually temporary, for the sea called. I imagine you can still work out a way to make a living afloat, though with more impediments than we encountered. Town, state, and federal regulations are around now that we never knew. They affect our lives and our pocketbooks. Something to take into consideration now is that things we thought nothing of doing in the past are now regulated. For instance, our small colony of cruising craft that laid up periodically in a backwater to lick wounds, refit, and make a stake to buy stores for another venture was left alone for the most part. Such operations are no longer tolerated in many places, and when they are, even their sewage discharge is spied on, charged for, and, at times, fined.

Some Conclusions   8

There comes a time when living aboard will no longer do. Whatever we do in this world must eventually come to an end, and we must face up to it. The end of anything can come for various reasons, and the end of our life afloat was no exception.

We had done and seen a lot, and enjoyed it. The income was sufficient to get along comfortably, but it was not enough to get ahead. The time came to think of the future, and quit while we could choose our time and place. There were other things we both wanted to do eventually. The mate had previous experience with horses, and she wanted to get involved with them again—she has a way with animals. I had ideas of setting up a small boatshop and eventually getting into design work.

We liked New England, and we would, when time and place suited, browse around ashore when we were on that part of the coast. The idea of a tomato patch, shingles overhead instead of decks, no anchors on our minds, and many other little things made us think of shore life. One fall, when we were about to head south again, we came upon the ideal house and shop on a side street—much overgrown and available. We had seen many places. This was it. We did not sail.

Naturally, all our goals for a new life were not reached in a minute, but we worked hard to make our land projects go. It was not pleasant to sell the vessel, but she could not be kept as a pet; she would run down from disuse. Retirement is the worst thing you can do to a still-able craft.

I know that discussing the end of one's life afloat is probably not what somebody considering going afloat wants to hear. I simply bring all this up to point out to anyone considering a life afloat that he should take into consideration the time when it will end. It is better to choose your own time to quit than to be driven into it by shipwreck, illness, or other mishap. You have a much better chance of coming out whole. I think in many ways we had pushed our luck far enough, and we knew it. There are lucky vessels—ours was one of them.

I constantly meet people considering such a life as we had, and they sometimes ask advice. When they talk of buying some 40-year-old vessel, I must play the Devil's Advocate and talk it down. A number of these craft have been along on some people's first and last voyage. They did not realize the craft needed total rebuilding, and usually did not have the skill or money to do it. I am sure old boats can be rebuilt—they have been successfully in the past and certainly can be in the future. But we must keep in mind that, though much has changed, the ability of the sea to pound some inadequate vessel to bits has not. By all means live on as good a craft as you can get. Even though you might manage to hold some crock together, she will nickel and dime you to distraction.

To quote costs and figures when we did live on the *Spray*, compared to now, does not mean much. Copper paint is no longer $3.00 a gallon in five-gallon lots. No one pays a skilled man in a shipyard 50 to 70 cents an hour, either. You can argue that the cost of living has gone up ten, twelve, or fifteen times what it was in my day, and then multiply my costs by that factor to get today's costs, but it's not as simple as that. I don't really understand inflation, anyhow, and it seems that even the experts can't come to any conclusion about it. To me, inflation simply means that more is less!

Life aboard boats has changed quite a bit since my day. You will have to contend with conditions, especially in this country but also in some foreign ones, that we never knew. Sewage disposal is one, and this can add to your running costs. We still don't seem to have the real answers to it, but you are supposed to abide by the rules. Some regulations for installing machinery and other mechanical and electrical gear on boats can add to your costs, too. How well any of these regulations can eventually be enforced we don't yet know. For commercial craft, I'm sure the new regulations are enforced now and will continue to be in the future.

Not every place welcomes live-aboard boats now, for various reasons. This makes life difficult, as you can't spend all your time at sea or in some desolate backwater. Yet there are also places that cater to live-aboards, and nowadays charge well for the privilege. There are some places that are free and easy as of old, but as time goes on they are fewer and fewer. Crowded ports and waterways are the wages of affluent society—many boats, owned by people who can afford them and who don't stay aboard for long periods.

Taxes of all kinds seem to be levied more and collected more diligently than they used to be. All boatyards, whether they like it or not, are having their prices forced up by the constant increase in wages, which of course affects every other thing you and your craft will require. I am sure it is hard for young people to picture how it was in the past, and maybe that's a good thing; they are accustomed to the present and very recent past, for they know no other.

For the cruising boat, I do not think the fuel difficulties will pose any long-term headaches. After all, in the not-so-distant past, all sailing craft had no machinery. Nonexistent oil I consider a small problem. A far worse menace is a government edict of some kind. It has almost come to the point that the government can tell you when and how to sail, and what canvas to carry, not that it knows anything about such subjects, of course.

That we lived afloat in a better era than now is open to argument. Besides, it's a meaningless argument. The thing is to do it when you can, and in the times you find yourself in. And be sure to do it when you are young enough.

What vessel you use will very much depend on the time you do it, too. Keep in mind, however, that the sea does not change, and, in spite of much dogma otherwise, a sea-keeping vessel's design has not changed much in a hundred years—in fact, many today are not as good as some of the round old things of the past. Many of the skills that were necessary for life afloat when I was doing it are still required today—I don't say that you have to have a craft anywhere nearly like the *Spray*, but you do need one that has at least some of her very great advantages. I am sure the very light displacement craft popular in some circles today are not what you want. They can be very tiring in many ways if you are on board them for long periods.

Working with tools, doing your own repairs, maintaining a self-sufficient world on board, learning where and when to buy supplies for both ship and self—all this is part of life afloat. How you make some income is, of course, important, and I can give little advice for the present. All things seem more organized than they used to be. There is more fuss and rule-making about taking a job—you are now a number and are being constantly checked on. It's even difficult to be a genuine bum now; our do-good government almost makes it impossible to be one, although, I suppose, if you work it right, it will pay you to be one.

My last exposure to charter work was in the 1960s, as a pro on a nice schooner. It seemed then, and perhaps even more so now, that chartering is much more of a rat race than it used to be. There seem to be hundreds of boats advertising for charter, and, though you can do fairly well if you know what you are doing, it takes a lot out of you and you must have frequent breaks. Besides being able to get along with most people (some few always being impossible), you must also set an excellent table at all times and on time. If there is no gripe about the grub, there is little else to fuss about.

Assuming that your chartering, or whatever you choose, will be more difficult than ours, at least in some ways, the axiom to keep things simple and easy to rebuild or repair still holds good, and always will. A complicated ship means more upkeep, both in work and in cost.

An overly long-legged craft has no advantage at all for the sort of life I have described, and many drawbacks. A good shoal-draft vessel could well have the most advantages. A boat with one of the modern odd-shaped underwater profiles would be unsuitable; beaching, where there is tide enough, hauling out, especially in out-of-the-way places, could be difficult and expensive, and an accidental grounding quite so.

Now, with all the new wonder materials, many will argue for a craft built of them. Whatever you use, keep in mind that it should be something quite possible to

repair in out-of-the-way places, even if it is a major job. This applies to all the vessel's gear and fittings, too, maybe more so.

Though many will not agree, I think, in selecting a vessel now, you should consider something based somewhat on the classic types, a design developed from the working craft of the past. If you buy a secondhand craft, get the very best and newest you can afford; it will save you money and many a headache in the end. Though there seems to be a return to more-or-less classic craft, good ones are not easy to find and are not cheap.

Having a new vessel built is expensive, especially if she is totally constructed by a yard. From my experience at the moment of writing, the best you can do in new, yard-built construction is about $2.50 per pound of displacement, and you have to shop for that. Often it can be arranged for a yard to finish the craft partly and you can do the rest, which works out better—sometimes—if you know what you are doing.

Speaking of displacement, 25,000 to 30,000 pounds is about all a young and able couple would want to handle and maintain on a regular basis, but there are exceptions. In my opinion, a boat of this size is now a little small for most charter work. Properly rigged, and handled by a strong and prime seaman, assisted by a mate willing to take her lumps, you can get by with a boat of 40,000 to 42,000 pounds displacement.

For living and working afloat, you have to be properly rigged. You have more than enough to do without having to fight some poor design of both vessel and gear. This is important, because the heavier the craft the more overhead there will be—more surface to sand, paint, and chase leaks on, a bigger power plant, both aloft and under deck. Though in some ways more comfortable and usually faster, the bigger boat can keep you humping.

I add one more thing—have a mate that can take it as well as dish it out, and if she has a cast-iron stomach, so much the better. She will work in a galley with a thermometer reading 100 degrees at times, and take a lonely wheel watch at night with frost on the deck once in a while. She will have to look after you when you are sick from exhaustion, and you will have to do the same for her. She will be frightened many times, and won't show it. More than once she will be fed up, especially with chartering. So use your head. After you have made a bit of money, spend it on a night out—fancy dinner and booze in keeping. She will feel much better. And when you can manage, take an occasional excursion away from the vessel for a short while.

Now, you go try and find a good vessel!

Index

Italic numbers indicate illustrations.

Accommodations, 26, 41-42, 76-85, *4, 78-79*; cabin, 26, 41-42, 78-80, 82, *4, 78-79*; forecastle, 77; galley, 80-82; lazarette, 83
Anchoring, 48-52, *49*
Anchors, 43-48, *45-46, 64*
Anti-fouling devices, 93-95

Ballast, 33
Batteries, 90-91
Bilges, 91
Blocks, 57
Boatbuilders, 11, 14-16, 22, *10, 18*; Alonzo R. Conley, 11, *10, 18*
Boatbuilding, 9-30
Boatyards, 12-13, *10*
Booms. *See* Spars
Bowers. *See* Anchors
Bowsprits, 65-66, *66*
Builders. *See* Boatbuilders
Building. *See* Boatbuilding
Bulwarks, 40, 64

Cabins, 26, 41-42, 78-80, 82, *4, 78-79*
Caulking, 23-26, *27*
Chafe prevention, 58
Chartering, 5-6, 108-112
Cockpits, 40-41
Compasses, 73-74
Conley, Alonzo R., 11, *10, 18*
Culler, R. D. (Pete), *118*; Toni, *71, 110, 118*

Deadeyes, 58, *59*
Decay, 98
Decks, 42
Depth sounders, 75-76
Dinghies. *See* Yawlboats
Dividers, 74

Engines, 85-90, 91-92, 101; exhaust system, 91-92; maintenance, 101
Equipment. *See* Gear
Exhaust systems, 91-92

Forecastles, 77
Framing up, 20-21, *19, 24-25*
Freighting, 117-120, *120*
Fuel storage, 71-72, 85

Gaffs. *See* Spars
Galley, 80-82
Gear, 43-72, 73, 98, 99; ground tackle, 43-52; horns, 69-70; lifelines, 64-65; lights, 70; navigation gear, 73-76; rigging, 57-58; sails, 58-62, 66-69; spars, 62-63, 65-66, 98, 99; steering gear, 52-53
Generators, 90
Ground tackle, 43-52, *45-47, 49*
Grounding systems, 91

Hauling out, 93-95, *94*
Heads. *See* Toilets
Horns, 69-70

Ice storage, 81

Jibs, 68

Kedge. See Anchors

Lanyards, 58, *59*
Launching, 26-30, *28-29*
Lazarettes, 83
Leadlines, 73
Leak prevention, 97-98
Lifelines, 64-65
Lights, 70, 90
Lines, *Spray*, 3
Living on board, 104-121
Lofting, 16-17
Logs, 75

Mainsails, 67-68
Maintenance, 93-103
Masts. See Spars
Mizzens, 68-69

Navigation gear, 73-76; compasses, 73-74; depth sounders, 75-76; dividers, 74; leadlines, 73; logs, 75; parallel rulers, 74; protractors, 74; radios, 75; RDFs, 75-76; sounding poles, 73; sextant, 73

Paint, 95, 97, 99-100; burning off, 97
Parallel rulers, 74
Passage making, 33-35
Planking, 23, *24*
Portholes, 82-83
Propeller shafts, 101-102
Protractors, 74
Purnell T. White, 26

Radios, 75
RDFs, 75-76
Rigging, 57-58; blocks, 57; chafe prevention, 58; deadeyes, 58; lanyards, 58; tackles, 58
Rudders, 52, 96-97

Sail plan, *Spray*, 2
Sailing, 31-43; singlehanded, 35; to windward, 31-32
Sails, 58-62, 66-69, *34, 60-61*; jibs, 68; mainsails, 67-68; mizzens, 68-69; topsails, 58-62, *34, 60-61*
Sawing wood, 19-20
Seaworthiness, 39-40, 42
Self-steering systems, 5, *23*
Sextants, 73
Shipyards. See Boatyards
Singlehanded sailing, 35
Sinks, 80
Sounding poles, 73
Spars, 62-63, 65-66, 98, 99, *66*; bowsprits, 65-66, *66*
Steering gear, 52-53, 96-97, *53-54*; rudders, 52, 96-97; tillers, 53
Stoves, 80, 102; maintenance, 102

Tackles, 58
Tenders. See Yawlboats
Tillers, 53
Toilets, 84-85
Tools, 100
Topsails, 58-62, *34, 60-61*

Water storage, 70-71, 83-84, *38*
Windlasses, *47*
Wood, 11-12, 19-20; sawing, 19-20

Yawlboats, 53-56, 102, *55-56, 86-87*